Build & Convert
Aviation Classics
Part 1

Edited By Gary Hatcher

SAM PUBLICATIONS

Build and Convert #6
Aviation Classics Part 1

Edited by Gary Hatcher

First produced in 2013 by Media House
21 Kingsway, Bedford, MK42 9BJ, United Kingdom

ISBN: 978-1-906959-31-9

Typeset by Media House, 21 Kingsway, Bedford, MK42 9BJ, United Kingdom
Designed by Jonathan Phillips
Printed and bound in the United Kingdom

Featuring the work of:
Will Alcott; Paul Bradley; Andy Brook; Peter Brown; Wojciech Butyrcz; Dick Clark; Brian M. Cooker; David Francis; Dave Hooper; Mike Jerram; Ross Marven; Angus McDonald; Neil Pinchbeck; Paul Stapleton; John Stokes; Matt Willis

SAM PUBLICATIONS

Contents

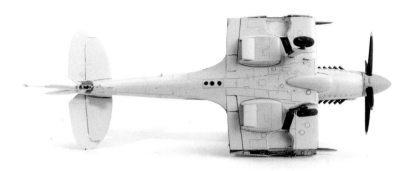

Introduction

Once again Build & Convert takes a journey through the Scale Aviation archives, this time bringing you a selection of aviation legends in scale, and offering a real cross-section of material from the best-selling magazine. Ranging from the Avro York to the Sopwith Pup, with rotary-winged and civil aviation for good measure, this latest compendium reflects not only the breadth and diversity of the magazine's contents, but also the eclectic nature of the Airfix catalogue, from which legendary repository the featured kits are drawn.

Gary Hatcher
Editor
Scale Aviation Modeller International

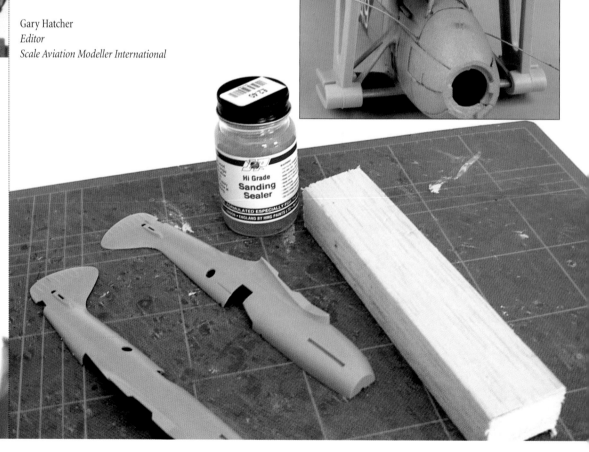

Chapter I

Airfix Kit 136

AVRO LANCASTER B MkI/III

Avro York
Rebuilding the Bus

An early airliner from a wartime bomber
By Angus McDonald

Designed to work with the Airfix Lancaster kit, CMR's Avro York conversion is a long-overdue and excellent rendition of this important transport aircraft.

The set includes a complete new fuselage, with resin pieces for all the portholes and a pair of vacform canopies. Vertical tail surfaces are included, as is a complete and comprehensive flight deck. New props and spinners are provided, and the instructions show clearly where the Airfix wings will need to be cut to fit the new fuselage.

Decals are provided for four machines: MW103; G-AGJA, a camouflaged York operating with BOAC in 1944; MW140 *Endeavour* in natural metal finish with either RAAF or RAF ferry flight markings; and G-ANTK, an ex-RAF machine still flying with Dan-Air in 1964 and now preserved at Duxford.

Somewhere in the dim and distant corners of my memory, I seem to recall getting involved in the production process of this kit. Only in a microscopic, vastly peripheral manner, mind you. Patience is the key with CMR releases, and the wait has been well worth it. Cast in their usual creamy coloured resin, the surfaces are smooth, virtually blemish free, carrying subtle detail, with engraved panel lines and raised features such as fairings, blisters and chutes. The detail is in the small parts, and they are wonderful. I was particularly taken by

AVRO YORK C 1 CONVERSION		
Scale: 1/72	Kit No: 136	
Status: New Tooling		
Type: Resin		
Parts: Resin 40, Clear 41, Vacformed Clear 2		
Decal Options: 4		
Manufacturer: CMR		
UK Importer: Hannants		

the delicate exhaust stubs, even more delicate horn balances for the rudders, and the throttles.

You need a donor Lancaster kit. Airfix is the natural choice, and the one recommended by CMR. It has the virtue of being relatively cheap and quite accurate, but has major fit problems. As the CMR York neared the end of its elephantine gestation period so the Hasegawa Lancaster became available and is also a suitable donor, albeit a rather expensive one.

Decisions, decisions
Before embarking on construction you must decide which aircraft you are going to build. If you chose the civilian version, the first thing to do is remove the exhausts from the engine nacelles. Airfix only

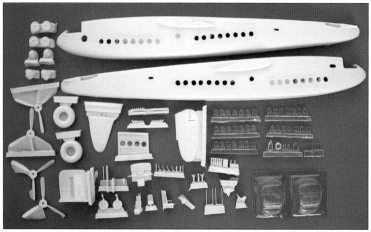

Comprehensive nature of the CMR conversion kit is evident here

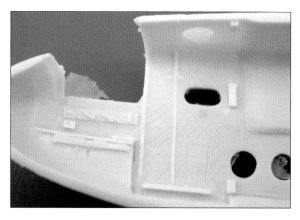

Cockpit sidewall detail

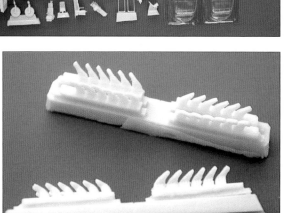

"I was particularly taken by the delicate exhaust stubs...

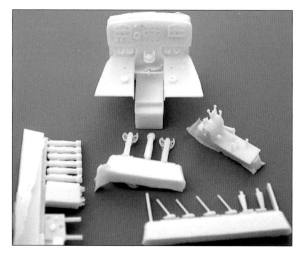

...and the even more delicate rudder horn balances and throttles"

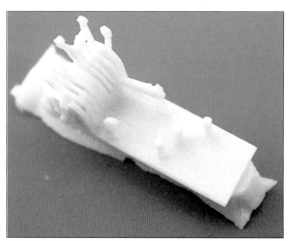

Angus devised a 'cunning plan' to address the wingroot area. "You can see that the curve is very subtle, but it makes a huge difference, and needed only a tiny amount of filler to make good the resulting small gap

"Masterpiece of engineering" cockpit components, little of which can be seen after assembly, were given "minimal cleaning up, with paint sort of splashed here and there"

provide the shrouded variety in the Lancaster kit, and virtually all the civilian versions of the York had unshrouded exhausts. I would recommend that you trim CMR's wonderful exhaust stacks from their pouring stubs and get them to fit the nacelles at this stage. It is far easier to cut any slots in the nacelles to accommodate the exhausts while they are in bits. I didn't, and had a merry time sanding the pouring stubs on eight exhausts until they were less than paper thin, removing most of my finger nails and fingerprints in the process.

Some of the aircraft will utilise the Airfix fins with the short trim tab, while others need CMR's fins (probably of more scale-like section than Airfix's thick ones) which have longer tabs.

Finally, I believe you will have to fill in the small rectangular windows near the tail for a couple of the colour schemes. I didn't, and it was only when I fitted the decals that I discovered something looked amiss and checked my references more closely. In true Bohemian style, I decided to leave well alone.

Wings and Nacelles

First job was to scribe selected panel lines on the Airfix wings and nacelles to match the engraved panel lines on the CMR parts. No great drama, over and done with relatively quickly and painlessly. Then some 9mm has to be removed from the wing roots. But wait! Do not commence hacking just yet. I digressed from CMR's instructions. They would have you cut the 9mm from the wingroots of both wing halves, join the wings to the fuselage, then use filler to make good the resulting large gaps. I felt I wasn't up to doing this and achieving the graceful curve where the wings join the fuselage. My cunning plan (beautifully executed I might add) was to cut 7mm off

The painting process is under way

the root of the top wing half and 9mm off the root off the bottom. I then scraped and cut and sanded the top wingroot until it fitted up against the fuselage. The process only took about half an hour per wing. The curve is very subtle, but it makes a huge difference. I needed a tiny amount of filler to make good the resulting small gap.

Next I embarked on the process of building the Airfix wings. This epic saga consisted of gluing the nacelles together, muttering, gluing the front of the engines onto the nacelles, swearing at the poor fit, gluing the nacelles onto the wings, much blaspheming, then several iterations of filling the Titanic gaps with various fillers (superglue, cement, putty, acrylic paint), muttering, much sanding, even more swearing. Repeat until all was blended together.

I also removed the blocks from the front of the carburettors and replaced them with fine mesh. Unfortunately I hadn't realised that the mesh was made of steel, and had a tricky job cutting, and a worse time gluing them into place. I am not pleased with the results.

The CMR Conversion

CMR use a relatively soft resin and go to great efforts to engineer pouring gates to be as small as possible. This means separating kit

Fuselage halves needed their mating edges cleaning up before joining, resulting in excellent final fit

parts from the stubs is relatively straightforward. However, in places your skills will be tested, such is the delicacy of their castings. I usually wash the parts to remove any of the silicon-based release agent, and the best 'detergent' I have found to do this is — wait for it, you won't believe it — Palmolive soap! It's so brilliant at cleaning release agents from plastic models. If it can do that with release agent, one wonders what it does to your delicate skin in the bath?

The fully fitted cockpit is a masterpiece of engineering. You can have a field day superdetailing the already wonderful level of detail provided. However, as I cleaned up the parts it dawned on me that

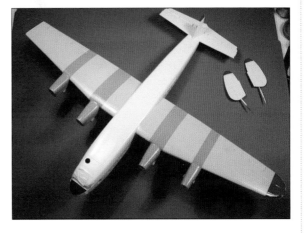

very little would be seen through the transparencies, especially all the stations behind the pilots' seats. Thus I did minimal cleaning up, and sort of splashed paint here and there.

The fuselage halves need their mating edges cleaning up before joining. Unlike previous CMR models that I have built, the cockpit parts needed no trimming to slot neatly into the fuselage, and the overall fit of the fuselage halves was equally excellent. There was a fair amount of trimming to get the Airfix tailplanes to fit the fuselage. The top surface shape didn't conform to any of the reference materials I had. In the end I smeared the area with filler and sanded everything smooth.

Many a cold dark night was spent fretting about what to do with those round fuselage windows. CMR provide clear resin parts for these, but I shied away from fitting them. It was the thought of all the trimming needed to get them to fit the fuselage, and then all the masking prior to painting. I took the easy route and used Kristal Klear once the model had been fully painted. Recently CMR have been providing clear resin cockpit canopies with their kits, but the one that came with my sample was of the vacformed variety. Thin, clear and easy to trim, it fitted the fuselage perfectly.

The undercarriage oleos and struts are courtesy of the Airfix kit. These were well moulded. The struts and oleos actually had a circular

cross-section, and detail was sharp. Minimal trimming was required to remove the seam lines before the whole lot got a coat of Halfords grey primer, followed by Halfords aluminium spray paint. My only contribution was to add the tiny black decals on the struts.

CMR provide a wonderful set of weighted wheels. Tread consists of the crosshatch pattern, while the hubs are separate pieces. The whole package certainly puts the kit's effort to shame, and effortlessly clicked into the Airfix undercarriage parts.

Painting and Decals

I decided on the striking Dan-Air scheme. All the more appropriate when I learned that Dan-Air once flew out of Blackbushe Airport, which is about a kilometre behind where I live.

I considered the acreage of white in the Dan-Air scheme, and then wondered what heinous crime I committed in a past life to end up doing so many aircraft recently with white colour schemes. Anyway, down went a coat of Halfords white plastic primer. Any defects were made good with blobs of acrylic paint and sanding, before another coat of white plastic primer to give the base colour. The whole aircraft was then sanded with 1200 grit wet 'n dry to smooth down the rough and knobbly finish imparted by the primer. Citadel blood red furnished all the red tips then the red and

Main landing gear is a combination of Airfix legs, CMR's excellent resin wheels and scratchbuilt door actuators

Tailwheel is CMR resin item

white parts were all masked off. Note the surfaces of the outer fins, which have a tiny sliver of a white line between the black and red. Masking them to the required thickness proved most industrious in the blaspheming department.

The instructions call for the engines and large strips across the wings to be coloured Dark Sea Grey. I noticed that Halfords grey primer was darker than it was six years ago, and I hoped that with the additional darkening effect of Johnson's Future/Klear varnish it would approximate to DSG. Well, it didn't. It was nearer to Ocean Grey. However, I have come across colour photographs showing weather-worn examples of the Dan-Air livery where the engines are suspiciously like Ocean Grey in colour. Apart from the black outer fins, the remainder of the fuselage was sprayed with LifeColor Light Compass Ghost Gray, lightened with Citadel skull white. A couple of coats of Future/Klear went down to prepare for the decals.

The decals are very thin, will not put up with rough handling and disintegrate without much provocation, especially the thin black line on the fuselage cheat lines. Unlike many offerings from the major kit manufacturers, these actually fit the model! This is particularly so for the cheatlines, which so often are just too short. Innovative as ever,

CMR have tried to make the modeller's life easy by providing cut-outs in the decals to fit around the nose and semi-circular pieces to fit over the fairing

Assembly of Airfix Lancaster kit's engine nacelles required liquid therapy of the non-cement kind, and alternate bouts of gluing and swearing

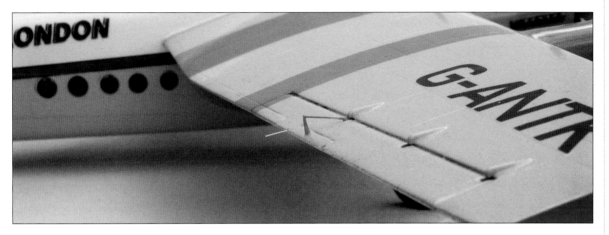

Angus scratchbuilt trim tab actuators and anti-static wicks

11

Vacform canopy was thin and fitted the fuselage perfectly, as seen here. For the York's 'porthole' cabin windows Angus preferred Kristal Klear to CMR's supplied clear resin inserts

CMR have tried to make the modeller's life easy by providing cut-outs in the decals to fit around the nose, and semicircular pieces to go over the fairings. This more or less worked, but not quite. Even so, everything nestled down nicely with Solvaset.

I was sorely tempted to do the wartime BOAC scheme, since the decals CMR supply for this scheme are wonderful. Unfortunately the BOAC aircraft had shrouded exhausts, and I had already cut off the Airfix kit's exhaust shrouds as I wanted to use the exhausts provided by CMR.

Final fitting Out

After my usual disasters spraying Future/Klear, necessitating much sanding, howls of frustration and many resprays, it was time to do all those fiddly bits which seem to take longer than constructing the major components. So in no particular order: cockpit framing was represented by strips of white decal. The astrodome was trimmed and fitted to the top of the fuselage. The excellent blister window slotted neatly into the fuselage side. Scratchbuilt aerial fitted above the cockpit. Framing for the sliding cockpit windows, plus resin window, stuck to the cockpit. Holes drilled into the fins to accept the horn balances, before fitting fins and horns, and I still managed not to fit them properly!

Scratchbuilt tab actuators for elevators and ailerons were fashioned to replace the parts provided by Airfix. Exhausts were painted and carefully stuck into place. CMR's excellent tailwheel, propellers and spinners were painted and installed. Main undercarriage along with doors and scratchbuilt door actuator struts followed. Carburettor grilles were glued in place, then reglued, and reglued as the blighters kept falling off. Fine stretched sprue was stuck into pre-drilled holes in the wing to represent anti-static wicks. The list was endless, and the process seemed to go on forever.

I attempted a bit of weathering, as the Merlins were particularly dirty, making nacelles and wings quite black. My usual weathering material of ground-up pastels wouldn't stick to the gloss finish, and with all the effort that went into this kit I didn't feel up to experimenting with spraying, so I reconciled myself with the fact that most photos I have of Yorks in civilian use show that the aircraft were quite clean.

And finally…

I love it. I love it. I love it! OK, you need a bit of old-fashioned modelling skill to hack the wings and get them to fit, but the rest of the kit is quite easy to put together. I would say that the Airfix components gave me the most grief, and required the greater amount of skill to get right. It's a crying shame that virtually none of the cockpit detail can be seen.

Pristine York

By Mike Jerram

Avro 685 York C.1 G-ANTK, as modelled by Angus McDonald, is one of two surviving examples in the UK. Built at Yeadon, near Leeds, in early 1946 it entered Royal Air Force service with 242 Squadron as MW232/KY-M. In June 1947, after two spells back at Avro for repairs following minor accidents, it was assigned to 511 Squadron at RAF, coded CJ, and took part in Operation Plainfare (Berlin Airlift) before sustaining further damage at RAF Gatow in January 1949. Repaired once more, it went into storage with 15 Maintenance Unit at RAF Wroughton and was refurbished at Ringway, Manchester by Fairey Aviation, who used it briefly for flight refuelling research before a further spell in store with 12 MU at RAF Kirkbride.

In July 1954 MW232 was disposed of on the civilian market and registered G-ANTK to Dan-Air Services Ltd, who operated the York as a freighter until 1964. Ferried to Dan-Air maintenance base at Lasham, Hampshire, it was used as a bunkhouse by the local Air Scouts troop until ten years later when the Dan-Air Preservation Group took on the task of restoring it. The Duxford Aviation Society (DAS) subsequently took over the project, and in May 1986 G-ANTK was transported by road to Duxford, where work continued.

After a 10-year restoration effort by DAS volunteers G-ANTK was rolled-out on 25 June 2006 resplendent in pristine Dan-Air livery, and for a few days shared the limelight (and sunlight) with Duxford's other preserved Avros — Anson, Lancaster, Vulcan and Avro Canada CF-100.

Thanks to Ellie Gittos of the Imperial War Museum Duxford for access to G-ANTK, and for her patience during a protracted photo session on a very hot ramp!

13

15

Chapter II

FAIREY SWORDFISH MK.I
Scale: 1/72
Kit No: 04053
Type: Injection Moulded Plastic
Manufacturer: Airfix
www.airfix.com

Airfix Kit 04053

Great Bags of String

A New-Tool Fairey Swordfish Mk I

By Dick Clark

Fuselage halves showing the control wires taped taut for painting

Airfix's new toolings get better and more ambitious with each new release. The company's all-new Fairey Swordfish has been hailed as possibly their best kit yet, ever. Possibly … but how does it turn out?

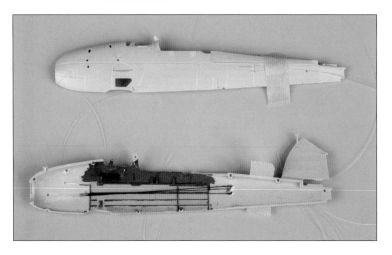

On first inspection it certainly looks promising. Highly detailed, well-moulded parts fill the box, together with a really good A4 instruction booklet and an excellent decal sheet. On closer inspection one discovers that the sprues are moulded in a rather soft, very light grey plastic, and while this soft material is undoubtedly easy to work with, it can be all-too-easy to mark it with tools or excess glue; also it doesn't lend itself to forming the finer parts. The instructions are not without errors and there are pitfalls along the way to trap the unwary.

The model can be regarded as several mini-kits in one, breaking down into four or five main sub-assemblies, which all come together as one progresses through construction. The first of these is the cockpit, which contains excellent detail in the self-contained main assembly as well as the moulded sidewalls.. One rather irritating aspect of the instructions is that, despite there being very good colour call-outs on the main full-colour painting guides, there is no such guide for the interior colours. This is all very well for experienced modellers, or those with references but not everyone will have these to hand. I thought the recommended colour for the cockpit sides, 61 'Flesh', a bit strange, so used a light creamy colour instead. This was my error, discovered too late, as the interior was wood painted with a protective varnish which gave it a reddish-brown tint. I still think Humbrol 'Flesh' is a bit odd,

The cockpit interior sub-assembly, painted and ready to insert in the fuselage, although the photo shows areas which need touching in

Note where the top of the armour-plate has had to be filed down to improve the fit.

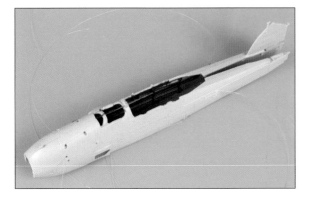

Stage 1 of joining the fuselage halves, with the forward upper join glued. At this stage the interior has not been added.

Stage 2, with the interior inserted, requiring clamping until thoroughly set before moving on.

17

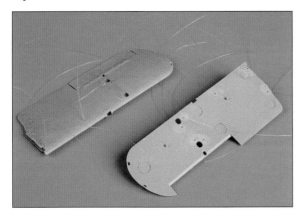

On the left, the starboard lower wing assembled with the rigging cables fixed. On the right is the upper half of the port lower wing, showing how the line is fixed from the inside, before the lower half is added.

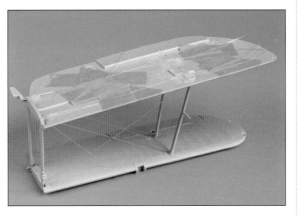

The port wing with struts and the lower half of the upper wing added, lines pulled taut and taped down, then fixed with CA glue

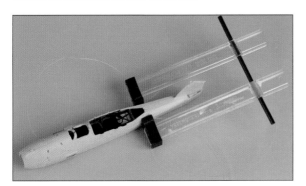

Stage 3, clamped further back to bring the rear upper join together. The tail section came together without trouble at this stage.

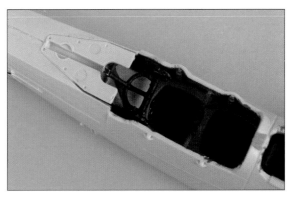

Showing the fit between the fuselage halves behind the cockpit and the resultant poor fit of the rear decking

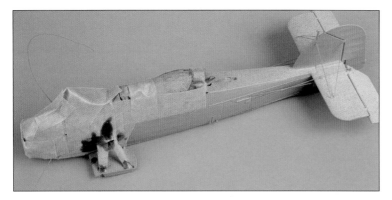

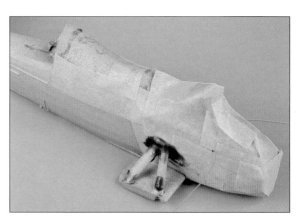

The fuselage after applying the Light Ghost Grey, masked up ready for spraying the Gloss Aluminium.

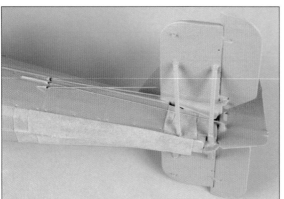

The liquid masking needs to be trimmed up - that blob on the wing-stub needs to be removed altogether, but it's better to let it set and then remove it than to try to clean it up when wet

The intricate masking under the tailplanes around the control wires and, yes, the tape does need burnishing down better prior to painting

Fitting the mid-upper wing section using the clever jigs supplied with the kit

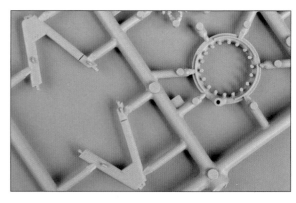

Don't be tempted to add the undercarriage struts before this stage, as the jigs will not then fit

Heavy sprue gates on the main undercarriage struts and the exhaust collector ring prevent these parts from being sprayed on the sprue

Assembling the main undercarriage struts fitted dry to the fuselage, thus allowing them to be removed for painting

Fuselage and wings completed as sub-assemblies prior to joining the whole lot up. Note that the blanking plates at the ends of the upper mid-wing section should not be fixed at this stage, as they serve to lock the upper wing hinge in position

but it is probably the nearest Humbrol match.

The interior is an awkward bit of construction, but it does help if part number 6A, in section 9, is not glued between its supports, so that its position can be adjusted later. The kit contains parts for an auxiliary fuel tank, which would fit on the cockpit floor in the observer's (i.e. centre) crew position. There is no mention of this in the instructions, so one assumes it is included for future releases, which is a pity because it is a valid option for a Mk I including, I believe, the Operation Judgement option included in this release.

For an aircraft that was famously nicknamed the 'Stringbag' it is a great shame that Airfix have not included any form of rigging diagram in the instructions. I personally could not contemplate a model of the type without rigging and so ordered a copy of *How To Build Tamiya's Fairey Swordfish*, by Geoff Coughlin, from Hannant's. Although this book refers to another maker's Swordfish kit, in 1/48, it is perfectly good as a reference guide to building Airfix's 1/72 version. The first major addition resulting from this was the control wires for the elevators and rudder. The fairings where these wires emerge from the side of the fuselage were drilled through and fishing line inserted and superglued to the forward section of the inner cockpit side. Painted black, these are visible through the cockpit opening, although you may have to take my word for that!

Next stage is to close up the fuselage halves with the cockpit sub-assembly trapped inside. Dry fitting showed this was not going to be a simple operation and I spent some time considering whether to follow the instructions, or to deviate from them by joining the fuselage halves, then inserting the cockpit assembly from below. In the end I went with the instructions, but not before spending some time filing the top of the instrument panel and the armour plate behind the pilot's seat to improve the fit. Even then the fuselage halves had to be glued in several stages, working from front to back, applying tape and clamps and allowing each stage to set thoroughly before moving on. Consequently this took a couple of days to achieve. Despite my best efforts there was still a poor join in the seam immediately behind the cockpit, which would come back to haunt me later.

While this was going on I began work on assembling and rigging the main wings. At

this stage one has to decide whether one wishes to build the kit with the wings open or folded, as the inner struts are different (and those for the folded option are not numbered on the sprue). Holes were drilled in the lower halves of the upper wings, and the upper halves of the lower wings (are you following?), and fishing line threaded through. This was superglued in place from the inside. Now the lower wing, struts and the lower half of the upper wing were assembled, after which the rigging was pulled taut, taped down and superglued in place. Once this was set the excess line was trimmed off and the upper half of the top wing glued in place. This stage required clamping with clothes-pegs, which may have been due to the slight extra thickness inside where the rigging had been glued in place. The rods connecting the cross of the front and rear main bracing wires (sorry, I don't know the technical name for it) were made from piano wire.

Now to return to the fuselage. The lower fuselage section, with the upper sections of the inboard lower wing stubs fixed, just about fitted properly, although it might have fitted better had it not been for the problems closing up the upper fuselage halves. Some filler was needed along the bottom seam behind the wing stubs. It's a good idea to mask up the small clear parts before adding the wing stub-to-fuselage struts. These struts are a very precise fit; I found I needed to locate the top first, then snap the wing locations in place, running liquid cement into the locations afterwards. I did not add the struts in front of the cockpit yet, skipping stages 18 and 19 to deal with the tail surfaces next. There are some sink-holes to be filled in part 14D.

I set the elevators at a slight droop, as seems to be common in photographs of parked Stringbags. Once the tail assembly has set the control wires can be fixed with CA glue, finishing off with the bracing wires,

Part 21A is a section of decking that fits behind the rear gunner's position, although owing to the difficulties I had encountered closing up the fuselage, this part fitted with quite a gap down one side. This was filled, but some of the intended detail here was lost in this process. The forward struts, parts 1 and 2B, were added, as well as the windscreen. I left the engine assembly, stages 20 through to 29, until right near the end of the build. This is the best stage to paint and decal the fuselage and wings.

The cockpit opening and the hole where the

engine assembly would attach were blocked up with tissue paper and everything given a coat of white auto primer. Next, the front and rear of the fuselage were sprayed with Tamiya AS-26 Light Ghost Grey. When this was dry a very tricky masking-up session ensued, working very carefully around the control cables under the tail and around the struts up at the front (liquid mask was needed around these struts). The instructions don't make it clear where the demarcation between grey and silver should lie beneath the cockpit; the side and underside elevations do not seem to match up, so a certain amount of guesswork is needed. Now the rest of the fuselage, and the wings, were sprayed with Tamiya TS-17 Gloss Aluminium. The masking must be removed with as much care as it was applied!

The whole lot was given a couple of coats of clear gloss in preparation for decaling. There are a few pitfalls with the decals. If one has opted for the camouflaged version, and you have added control wires as I have, you will encounter problems with the fuselage roundels as they need to go under the wires where they enter the fuselage. You may need to cut the roundels into sections, or maybe cut slits to go past the wires, before soaking the decals. With this version, the wide blue

stripes across the fuselage sides do not fit well over the upper cockpit sides, requiring a lot of softening and setting solution and, even then, I found they needed to be cut to fit properly, and touched in when dry. Another problem was encountered with the large '649' decals under the upper wing, which do not fit outside the outer struts as I expected them to. The struts want to go inside the '6'.. If that is how they are supposed to fit, then the decals really should have been designed in two halves. I compromised, cutting the '6' away from the '49' and locating it inside the struts.

When the decals were set they were given a brush-applied protective coat of Klear, then the panel lines given a mid-grey wash. I was trying for a fairly weather-worn look for this model. Finally all was given a coat of semi-matt varnish, and it was back to construction, putting all the sub-assemblies and final details together.

If one is building the model with wings folded as here, skip stages 38 through to 46.

I assembled and pre-painted the upper mid wing section before fitting it to the fuselage using the very clever jigs provided to set the correct angle and spacing (though I'd give it a lot longer than the

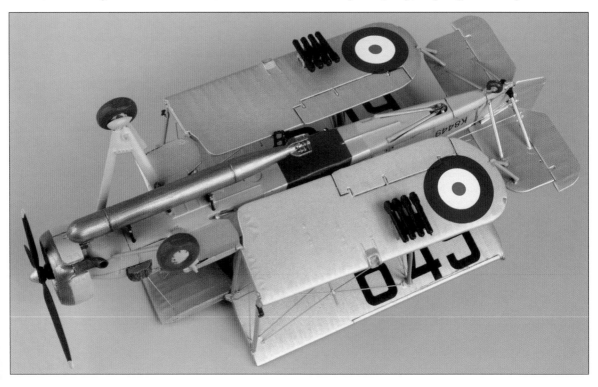

recommended 1 hour to set). Note that the decal does not fit well over the mouldings on top of the wing section, even with copious amounts of setting solution. You may find it an awful lot easier to mask and paint the St Andrews Cross than to use the decal.

Do not make the mistake I did. Do not add the upper wing stub blanking plates, parts 6 & 7B, before fixing the wings! Follow the instructions and brush-paint the blanking plates after fixing.

Also, do not try to add rigging between the fuselage and upper mid-wing section before adding the main wings, otherwise you're likely to pull the first side too tight and not realise until you do come to fit the main wings. How do I know this? Hmm…

Suffice to say, these wires had to be cut and several more attempts made to add them satisfactorily … but more of that later.

It would have been great to have been able to spray the undercarriage legs whilst they were still attached to the sprue, but alas, the sprue gates are far too chunky. This is an issue with the whole kit, but more so with these smaller, more delicate parts, including some of the engine components. The solution was to cut them off, clean them up and assemble them by gluing the legs together fitted dry to the fuselage, then remove them, paint them and finally refit them with CA glue to the fuselage. The wheels fit on square lugs ensuring that their flats set at the correct angle. The tyres were painted with Granite Grey, as tyres on naval aircraft of this period faded quickly from black due to the effects of the salt-laden air. Add the oil cooler and the crank handle either side of the forward fuselage, and that's that.

At this stage I went back to step 20 to 29 in the instructions, dealing with the engine and prop as another sub-assembly. The Tamiya Swordfish book is an invaluable aid here, allowing accurate detail painting of the well-moulded engine. I followed stages 21 to 25 and painted the cowl assembly at this point, undercoating in white, then spraying Light Ghost Grey to the outside of the cowling. The inner surface, crankcase and its mounts were painted with acrylic semi-matt black, the exhaust collector-ring with Citadel Bolt-gun Metal, and the exhaust stubs and pipe picked out in various rusty browns. Fitting the engine to the crankcase is rather tricky as its locating lug is minute; in the end I removed the lug and aligned the cylinder heads with the exhaust stubs. This complete sub-assembly was then fitted to the fuselage and the propeller added to finish.

The wings were finished by adding the small bomb-racks and bombs, and the torpedo was fitted under the fuselage. Incidentally, the Tamiya book tells us that red-topped torpedoes were practice rounds, so not appropriate for a machine armed for an active mission. This gave me three final sub-assemblies of fuselage and both main wings.

Now, hopefully you haven't made the same mistake I did, and you haven't already added the blanking plates to the upper wing centre-

section. You're supposed to fit these after fitting the outer wings, as they serve to lock the upper hinge in place. Ho hum. The wings are a bit flimsy until you add the retaining hook frames underneath the tailplanes. I believe the hooks on these are moulded the wrong way round. Just turn the frames round; no one will notice.

Be aware that frame part number 4B in the instructions is actually part number 5B on the sprue. Also there is no instruction as to what colour to paint these frames; you'll have to guess or refer to sources. For some reason I can't fathom, my port wing ended up slightly higher at the tip than the starboard wing, necessitating a little cheating, cutting the hook frame short on this side.

The last job - it took me another four attempts to get those front bracing wires remotely tight. Grrrr.

This is a very good model, but not one for the beginner or the faint-hearted. It fought me all the way and needs a lot to get the best out of it. But given the patience and dedication, this kit has the potential to deliver a really, really good model of the famous Stringbag in the classic 1/72 scale.

BE12a
A Scratch Conversion in 1/72

By Matt Willis

RE8
Scale: 1/72
Kit No: 01076
Type: Injection Moulded Plastic
Manufacturer: Airfix
www.airfix.com

The BE12a is one of the multitude of First World War aircraft that seem to have faded into almost total obscurity. Indeed, it is one of those aircraft that seems to have got virtually everything wrong. For a start, it was based on the derided BE2 series. Secondly, the BE12 'a' variant was kept aloft by the feared and hated unequal-span wings pioneered by the BE2e, and also seen on the RE8, which legend had it would crumple when not handled with kid gloves. Finally, it had on occasion to be pressed into service as a fighting aeroplane when air combat had barely been considered in the aircraft's design.

In fact, the BE12a was a more successful aircraft than reputation would suggest. It had the most success in combat against enemy aeroplanes out of the BE12 series (admittedly not a difficult record to beat) and in carrying out some useful bombing and reconnaissance work in Palestine and Macedonia, at least can be said to have freed up better machines for the harder-fought Western Front.

The first germ of an idea to build a BE12a came when considering what to tackle for the Airfix Tribute Forum's fourth anniversary group build. The site's anniversary builds offer the chance to build anything you like as long as the final build comprises at least 51% of an Airfix-boxed kit. It's an opportunity to do something a bit different, be creative, and share the work with other modellers of a similar bent. Previous projects in anniversary builds include complex conversions such as the transformation of the Short Sunderland kit

The cockpit floor and framework prior to fitting, with excellent Eduard seat

into a C-Class flying boat, or construction of rare and unusual kits like the Orion space shuttle from 2001: A Space Odyssey, to name but two. I wanted to build something obscure, that many people may not have seen before. The notion of a BE12a arose when I realised that the aircraft shared some major components with the RE8 - and Airfix had recently re-released its 1958-vintage 1/72 kit with fantastic new box art by Adam Tooby. The wings, tailplanes and engine were common to both types which, with a little creativity, gave me both a new and interesting subject and enough Airfix plastic to fit within the rules.

To start with, I made some rough plans for how to proceed. The Windsock Datafile (No.66) on the BE12/a/b provided some excellent plans and a plethora of photographs. This allowed me to choose a subject aircraft - A582 of 50 Squadron, on anti-Zeppelin duty at Detling in 1917 - and to help me assess how the build could be taken forward. It transpired that the forward part of the fuselage back to the rear of the pilot's cockpit could be retained with some tweaks, while the rear half of the fuselage would have to be created from scratch. The wings were a more straightforward proposition although consulting references showed that Airfix had simplified the lower wing's attachment to the fuselage somewhat. In addition, the upper wing was a little long and both wings' tips were a little too raked. This meant a few amendments to the wings would be necessary for accuracy's sake but in general the flying surfaces represented the easy bit - for now, at any rate.

The scratchbuilt instrument panel and wood/linen effect paintwork

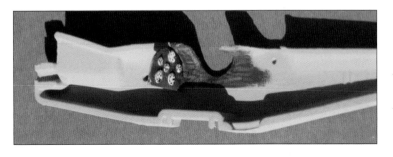

The order of the build presented some difficulties. I needed to assemble and paint the cockpit interior before the scratchbuilt rear fuselage could be added to the Airfix nose - potentially meaning that the join would be obvious. The answer was to fashion the sticks-and-wire version of a modern cockpit 'tub' - a false floor with fuselage framing built in that would slot into the interior and mask the junction between front and rear sections. This was constructed with Plasticard and square-section stock to form the longerons and uprights, with stretched sprue for bracing wires. The Airfix kit has no interior at all, save for two figures who sit on shelves. I removed these, added an instrument panel from Plasticard, punching discs of card to use as instrument faces. I painted the fuselage sides, and the cockpit 'tub', buff to represent the inside of the fabric covering, and any plywood sections were then overpainted with burnt umber oil paint, streaked with a brush, to create a wood effect. This is the most effective way I've found to create a realistic wood finish and with a little practice and experimentation it can be made to work very well. This technique served for all the wooden parts of the aircraft including the propeller, struts, and undercarriage.

The pièce de résistance of the interior was a pre-painted photo-etched seat from a set produced by Eduard. These are a brilliant innovation and represent the idiosyncratic RFC wicker seats to a tee.

As mentioned previously, the nose needs some modification as the RE8 had a 'kink' in the cowling line when viewed from above while the BE12a fuselage is a smooth line from nose to tail. The void was filled with Milliput and shaped according to photographs and plans.

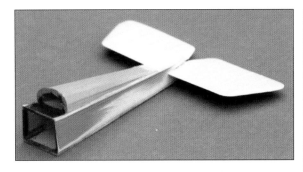

The Plasticard rear fuselage with RE8 decking and tailplanes

This is where things got experimental. I thought the rear fuselage needed work to make it look more like a single cohesive structure. I also wanted to reflect many photographs of BE12 types showing very wrinkled fabric. After considering several materials, I selected cigarette paper (Rizzla Red, if anyone's interested) and cut sections of this to conform to the model. A thin layer of slow-drying superglue was added to each surface and the paper applied. I then pulled the corners of the paper tight until the wrinkles were to my liking. Fortunately the effect was quite realistic.

The tailplanes were almost the right shape as they were, just needing some adjustment at the root to fit the scratchbuilt fuselage. The fin and rudder were totally different to the RE8 items, however, so new ones were cut from Plasticard with ribs from stretched sprue added.

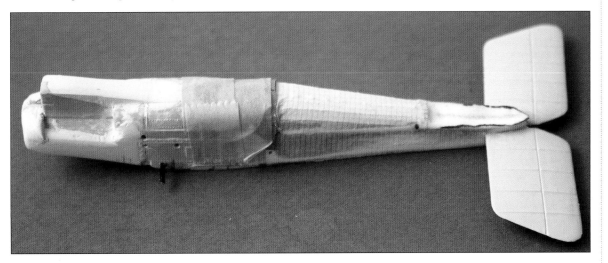

The rear fuselage now attached to the nose, which has had its profile altered with Milliput. Note the stub wing spar of copper wire

If I were to repeat this build I would do this before tackling the interior and joining the halves as it took great care to avoid the interior getting damaged or dirty. The air scoop between the cylinders also needed lengthening as on the BE12a the scoop faired into a fuel tank behind the engine and the slope finished approximately 5mm ahead of the cockpit opening. This was also done with Milliput.

The next task was the rear fuselage. This was a simple box-section of Plasticard with square section stock in the corners for reinforcement, made according to the plans in the Datafile. The BE2/12 family have a rather odd feature in this area in that the rounded rear fuselage decking terminates early, leaving a flat section ahead of the tailplanes and a 'broken backed' appearance. The reason for this is that the original BE1 had a very long-chord lifting tailplane and while this was later substituted for a more conventional short chord example, the fuselage was never modified throughout the entire production run of the BE family - even on ostensibly new types like the BE12a. The decking in question was carefully removed from the RE8 rear fuselage, shortened and attached to the new Plasticard structure.

The top wing was the most straightforward part of the whole build. The only modifications required were to remove a small amount from the tips, with a little less rake, to match the Datafile plans and to add a gravity tank (purloined from a DH2 kit). Similar alterations were made to the tips of the lower wings but the roots were a little more complicated as there should be a gap between the wing and the fuselage bridged only by the exposed spars. The simplest way to rework this area was to glue the one-piece lower wing in place then slice each wing off at the centre section, which was then filed to the right shape for the BE12a. Another 2mm was then removed from the root and small holes drilled at the spar locations in the wing roots and fuselage. In fact, the rear spar passed underneath the fuselage. For the forward spar I hit on the idea of using some thick copper wire used for 'training' bonsai trees. This was of scale thickness and allowed me to set the dihedral precisely, while for the rear spar I used Evergreen rod. The Airfix wing struts were over thick, so I cut new ones from Aeroclub strut stock - much more scale but less strong. The 'V' undercarriage was usable with some cleaning up and adjustment of the angles. On aircraft in the BE series the front leg of the 'V' type undercarriage did not attach directly to the fuselage

but to a small stub with an aerofoil fairing. This was represented with small pieces of strut stock.

The main assemblies were painted while still separate. The undersurfaces were sprayed ivory to represent clear doped linen, while the upper surfaces were airbrushed rust brown for PC12. BE12as were painted either PC10 or PC12 and it's impossible to tell from available images which is which, so you pay your money and take your choice. I went for the less obvious option as it seemed to fit the nature of the build. Cowling colours are equally uncertain. Most seem to be painted grey or the same colour as the rest of the airframe, but some seem to be natural metal, which I went for as A582 looked to have unpainted panels. This area was masked, primed with gloss black, and airbrushed with Alclad 'polished aluminium'. Decals were from Pegasus sheets of WW1 serials and roundels.

With all the major assemblies complete it was time to start bringing them all together. For all biplane models I use the Aeroclub assembly jig - a device I could not do without. It allows the modeller to set the

The BE12a mounted in the Aeroclub jig, invaluable for wing alignment

The model during wing alignment - the wrinkled and uneven fuselage fabric can be seen here

incidence, stagger and gap of biplane wings precisely. I started rigging the wings with 3lb monofilament fishing line when the model was in the jig, to ensure strength and rigidity as I was not convinced my new struts were man enough to hold everything together. The remainder of the rigging was completed when the glue on the struts had dried and the model had been removed from the jig.

The rigging on the BE12a is nothing short of a cat's cradle, with wires extending out to the long top wing overhang and across the top of the wing by way of inverted 'v' kingposts, which I modified from spare Nieuport 28 undercarriage struts. Despite the complexity, rigging was not as fiddly as it might seem. Because the rigging runs through the upper wing, holes could be drilled right through and long lengths of fishing line run through the holes and around the kingposts - I found this simpler than many biplanes where lots of short pieces of wire have to be secured. A hole right through the wing provides plenty of surface area for glue to attach the line. I stuck to my usual principle when rigging biplanes of including around 80 per cent of the wires as more than this can look too crowded.

Other than the rigging, there were a multitude of details to add. Like Many First World War biplanes, the BE12a seems to be covered in bits and pieces. The armament of one Lewis gun, on a hinged pole firing over the centre section, and a Vickers gun with Challenger gear on the fuselage side, were added with Aeroclub white metal guns, styrene stock and stretched sprue. An external rack for Lewis gun drums was made from Plasticard with drums made from grooved

slices of sprue. Control horns were donated from a Revell DH2, and exhaust stacks were based on the kit items modified from an 'L' shape to a 'Y' shape with Aeroclub tube. The characteristic, clumsy tailskid was made from a piece of right-angled strut from the spares box and plastic rod, with fishing line representing the bungee chord springing.

This was a complicated but very rewarding build resulting in a unique model which undoubtedly helped me develop as a modeller. It has given me the confidence to try some more ambitious builds - perhaps a BE2e next, or an FE9 perhaps...

25

FAIREY BATTLE
Scale: 1/72
Kit No: 03032
Type: Injection Moulded Plastic
Manufacturer: Airfix
www.airfix.com

The completed corrections give a better look to the model

Valiant Wings
Fairey Battle Corrections

By Paul Bradley

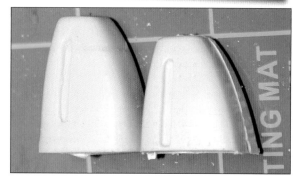

The Airfix Fairey Battle is another of those oft-reviled early Airfix kits, renowned for its inaccuracies. The story is that, back in 1968 when Airfix first proposed this kit, Fairey supplied them with the wrong set of plans – those for the design before its final shape was fixed and so not reflective of production airframes. Once the error was discovered by aviation historian and modeller, the late Ian Huntley - a Fairey employee at the time - Airfix were apparently livid, though it was too late in the process to do anything about it and so the flawed Battle lives on. Recently re-released, it now features a brand-new decal sheet featuring aircraft of the Hellenic Air Force and of 63 Sqn RAF.

So what's wrong with it? Basically, there are a number of major errors. The nose is 4mm too short, the outer wing chord is too narrow, the tailplanes are too small and the fin and rudder are both incorrect. The canopy arrangement is also not quite right. All this was ascertained by reference to the SAM Publications' *Aviation Guide to the Fairey Battle*. So why bother with it? Well, it is the only readily available Battle, the 2001 MPM kit being quite scarce and, perforce, not inexpensive. A check inside this new re-issue shows that the moulds have survived quite well, with just a touch of flash and no other major moulding flaws apparent. The surface detail is fine raised lines and rivets, all of which were removed before some re-scribing was done.

The first correction I did was to the fin/rudder. I marked the correct

Correcting the tail – a new rudder line, front and back

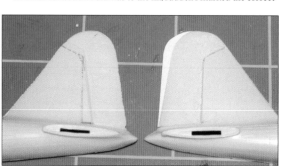

The Valiant Resin nose adds the missing 4mm behind the exhaust recess

rudder line in pencil before scribing, then filled the old rudder line with filler. The new rudder trailing edge was fashioned from some 10 thou plastic card and glued to the inner face of the starboard fin/rudder unit. Once the fuselage was joined, this was blended in with filler. A similar technique was used to get the correct wing trailing edge line. In this case, the leading edge is fine, but the trailing edge is some 3mm too narrow in chord at the outer edge of the aileron. The kit's ailerons themselves are pretty pathetic, so I ditched them and filled in the gaps, the corrective plastic card inserts providing a base for this. The new ailerons were scribed on later.

Another issue with the kit is the rear canopy, which does not depict the correct window pattern over the gunner's position. I used a Falcon vacform canopy, which does include the requisite panes, and trimmed the kit to fit.

The final major correction, and the raison d'etre of this review, was the nose. Valiant Wings' new resin part is cleanly cast with fine engraved detail, so you'll probably want to rescribe the rest of the model to match, as I did. It has the extra 4mm added at the rear of the part. As with the Stirling, I used a razor saw and mitre box to cut off the kit's nose cleanly at the panel line just aft of the recess for the exhausts. I soon discovered that the kit part narrows towards the

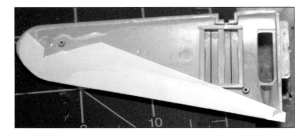

Adding a slice of 10 thou card in between the wing halves to follow the correct outline

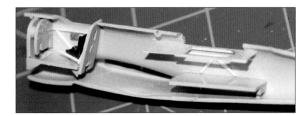

A basic interior using plastic card and rod. The PE seat is from an Airwaves Firefly fret

The card was layered with filler to produce the new trailing edge, and the ailerons filled then re-scribed later

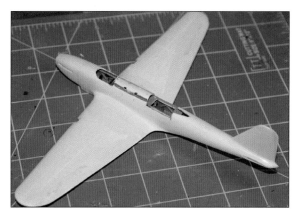

The basic airframe completed. Note the skylights in the inter-cabin coaming

bottom of the fuselage, which is also incorrect – I corrected this with a tapered spacer of 40 thou plastic card between the two halves of the lower lip of the intake, which forced apart the fuselage the appropriate amount.

I added some basic detailing to the fuselage interior, though not much will be seen once complete, then closed up the fuselage. The resin nose was butt-joined to the kit and it fit quite well; only a small amount of filler was used to blend it in. The exhausts were modified to represent the early 'kidney-style'. While I was working on the fuselage, I added the four small skylights in the coaming between the cockpits that Airfix missed.

The fit of the wings is very good, but I needed to trim a little from the fuselage slots to ensure this. The tailplanes are slightly undersized, but I decided not to correct these, as I personally didn't feel the effort was worth it – your mileage may vary.

The kit's undercarriage is a reasonable depiction, but the main wheels are too small and were replaced from my spares box, while the mudguards are much too thick, so I made new ones from 10 thou.

A quick coat of primer revealed some minor flaws to correct, mainly in my new ailerons. Once these were tidied up, I sprayed a coat of Dark Earth, followed by the camo pattern of Dark Green, then Black on the undersides. Next came a coat of Future, prior to decaling. I used the kit decals for 63 Squadron and these went down well with minimal silvering.

The vacform canopies were given strips of appropriately painted decal film to depict the framing, and coated with Future to seal them

in, and once dry, the canopies were attached with Contacta; the fit is not brilliant and some white glue was added as filler.

Compared to an unaltered Battle model, this one does look a lot better. The new nose makes a significant difference, but you'll wish to consider doing the other corrections for the most accurate model.

The kit wheels are too small – I found replacements in my spares box. Note also the re-shaped 'kidney-style' exhaust

27

Chapter III

GRUMMAN FM-2/WILDCAT VI
Scale: 1/72
Kit No: 10050
Type: Injection Moulded Plastic
Manufacturer: Airfix

Airfix Kit 10050

Wild-X-Cats
Grumman Wildcat

Making a Mountain out of a Molehill –
a Prototype Conversion

by Brian M. Cooker

The age of the biplane fighter was essentially over by the mid-1930s, but some companies persisted in developing aircraft using this time-tested design concept. Grumman was one of these firms, and why not? They had a track record of successful designs in the FF through F3F for the US Navy, and they were holding their own against strong rival companies. When the US Navy held a design competition to procure a follow-on fighter to the F3F in 1936, Grumman submitted drawings for the XF4F-1 biplane. Realising the competition was submitting monoplane designs, Grumman asked for and was granted an extension to resubmit their entry. The XF4F-2

The photograph that could never be taken in reality. Wildcat 0383 in its distinctive XF4F-2 and XF4F-3 configurations

was Grumman's monoplane answer to the Brewster and Seversky designs. Engine problems in the XF4F allowed Brewster's F2A Buffalo to win the production contract, but the new Grumman type showed sufficient potential to warrant funds for continued development. The F4F Wildcat series ultimately surpassed the Buffalo, serving with distinction throughout WWII. The Wildcat may not have been as sleek or manoeuvrable as its foes, but it had the advantage of being incredibly rugged and dependable.

XF4Fs

From a modelling point of view, prototypes have always intrigued me. Not only because they are seldom produced in model form, but also because they are often very different from the main production versions. The XF4F is one of these oddities. Few aircraft that I can recall have gone through as many noticeable configuration changes as did the Wildcat during its progression from paper to production. The evolution from the XF4F-2 to the production F4F-3 offers the opportunity to model some distinctive profiles that will add variety to your straight-from-the-box collection.

Cockpit and wheel well structure made from 40thou sheet

Control surface rib detail. The headrest was punched from 10thou sheet

The cowling for the XF4F-2 was taken from the Airfix Dauntless kit

Fuselage ready for closure. All interior surfaces were painted with Testors Flat Aluminum

Mass balances made from thin copper wire for the -2 only. The tips were coated with superglue to produce a tear drop effect

The Airfix Dauntless cowling mounted on a Dremel tool ready to be sanded into shape

Choosing the Subject

I decided to model both the XF4F-2 and the early XF4F-3, but to do so, some serious surgery was required. The kit manufacturers have not ignored the Wildcat, so there are plenty of options to provide a base for these significant but not too difficult conversions. My collection is exclusively 1/72 and includes all of the kits listed. Unfortunately, I was faced with a dilemma. Do I cut up and quite possibly ruin a perfectly good Hasegawa kit or do I attempt to reconstruct one of my ancient renditions that is clearly outclassed by the newer kits? I finally opted for the Airfix offering of the FM-2/Wildcat VI. I had several reasons for this choice: (1) I had two of them, built many years ago with more youthful enthusiasm than skill, (2) this kit has many shortfalls in detail and fidelity of scale which require some (a lot of?) work to bring it up to snuff, unless you are creating a Guadalcanal scrapyard diorama, and (3) if the attempt to modify them failed, I would have lost only $1.00 worth of plastic and not $15.00! Regardless of your choice, all of the currently available models will require the modifications described in this article to produce a prototype Wildcat, so do not lose sleep over trying to find a particular company's kit.

The Conversion Process

The transition from your base kit to the XF4F-2 and early XF4F-3 (hereafter referred to as the -2 and -3, respectively) will follow similar paths. Since there is so much in common, I will treat them together noting the -2 and -3 differences as we go.

Step 1: The Fuselage and Cockpit

The most significant modifications are required in the fuselage. Due to the extent of the changes and the addition of scratchbuilt sections, I opted to remove completely all surface detail provided by the kit. Start the alteration process by cutting off the upper spine at the seam and trimming it down to the shape shown in Figure 1. I scored the crease between the spine and the fuselage with a knife and carefully twisted the spine section until it broke free. Remove and discard the fin and rudder. After joining the two halves of the remaining spine, it will be re-attached between the fuselage halves just aft of the cockpit and rotated down at the fin, leaving no vertical spine showing at the junction. You will have to trim some of the fuselage wall just aft of the cockpit to make sure the spine fits without expanding the width of the fuselage.

XF4F-2 profile. Note the antenna mast is vertical but leans to the left

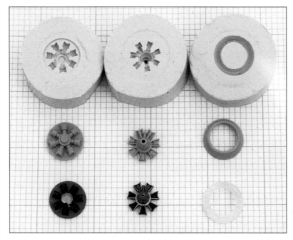

RTV moulds, Hasegawa kit parts and resin cast copies

Oil coolers on both wings and angled, more streamlined exhaust stacks on the XF4F-3

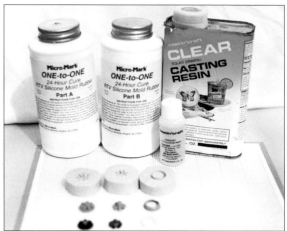

Casting materials used to duplicate kit parts

Single oil cooler scoop and vertical exhaust stacks on the XF4F-2

The XF4F-2 wing span was 34ft. Note the raised channels on both sides of the wings

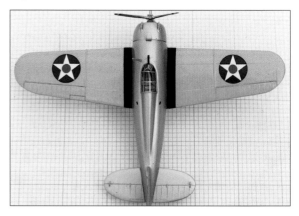

The finished XF4F-2 with long span ailerons and trim tab on the port side only

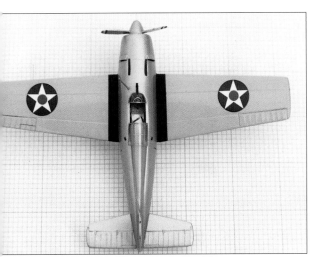

XF4F-3 with squared off wing tips, shorter (but still longer than production) ailerons and trim tab on the port side only

Both versions have semi-circular indentations in the rear bulkhead for the wheels. Note the extra window for both versions and single cowl flap for the -3 only

By using most of the kit's original spine, you retain the basic curves and reduce the need for excessive putty. For the -2 only, cut the forward fuselage approximately 1/8in (3.25mm) forward of the wing leading edge, insert a new firewall and round the edges slightly to present a noticeable break between the fuselage and the cowling. Even if you do not desire to superdetail the interior, some additional bulkheads made from 40thou styrene sheet are recommended. Figure 2 provides templates for the various bulkheads with 1 being the

Wheel indentation detail

forward firewall and 2, 2a, and 3 following aft. Position bulkhead 2 flush with the rear gear door opening with 2a immediately behind to double the thickness. The reason for this will be explained in step 4. Bridge the distance between bulkheads 1 and 2 to form a wheel well compartment ceiling. This ceiling should be just above the wheel opening and the full width of the fuselage. Next, cut a cockpit floor to span from bulkheads 2a to 3.

The real Wildcats had narrow foot troughs which left clearance on either side to allow the pilot to look down through windows in the belly. I made the floor slightly wider than the seat. Taking a cue from some aftermarket brass detail sets, I made a seat from an aluminium beverage can. [Figure 3]. The aluminium is easy to work with, it takes paint and superglue well and is cheap and readily available.

Before I glued the cockpit and wheel well enclosure to the fuselage, I cut extra belly windows for both the -2 and -3. The new window opening should be the same size as the existing window and located just above it. I made the windows themselves from Squadron's Clear 10thou thermaform clear plastic and attached them with Plastruct Plastic Weld. I have found this liquid cement does not craze most clear plastics when used sparingly, and as a bonus, it has extra 'body' that acts as a gap filler. I also added two

side consoles made of aluminium, as per Figure 3, which were superglued to the cockpit wall. Add the instrument panel and complete any other cockpit and wheel well detailing that will not be easily accessible after the fuselage halves are joined. Make a fuel tank from thin styrene sheet and attach it under the seat, midway between bulkheads 2a and 3. At this point, glue the cockpit enclosure to one fuselage half and add the cut-down spine and support behind bulkhead 3. Trim the spine and its support as required to get the correct angle and fit. Make a new fin and rudder out of 60thou sheet styrene. Figure 4 shows the profiles for the round -2 and the more angular -3. Note: The drawing indicates the total height of the fin/rudder. Since the exact position and alignment of the fin support may vary, cut the new fin/rudder slightly longer than required. Trim to the proper angle and height after the spine support is glued to the fuselage half. Scribe the fin/rudder and trim tab hinge lines. Join the fuselage halves together and fill the gaps between the fuselage halves and the spine, tapering the fin joint with filler.

Using the templates in Figure 5, make the horizontal tailplanes for the version(s) of your choice from 60thou sheet. Round or taper the appropriate edges and scribe the hinge and trim tab lines. The reshaped stabilisers for both the -2 and -3 are mounted low, directly to the fuselage. The elevator hinges were made from pieces of 5thou strip styrene. Do not go crazy over the elevator's and rudder's fabric surfaces. The rib detail is very subtle and may be left smooth, or if you are adventurous, try the technique described below (See sub-section: Fabric). Next, for the -2 only, add elevator counter balances made of thin copper wire . After bending the wire, I coated the tip with superglue to get the teardrop shape required. For the -3, the stabilisers have a slightly more swept-back leading edge than the production version and do not have the mass balances.

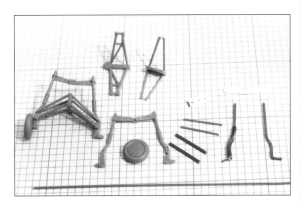

Hasegawa landing gear and scratchbuilt duplicate parts

The prototypes had solid rubber tail wheels, see Figure 7 also

The XF4F-2 had an angled, flat plate wind screen

The XF4F-3 had a circular, unbraced wind screen

New canopies were vac-formed using the kit canopy modified with filler. Plaster of Paris was added to prevent distortion during the vac-form process. Shown is the XF4F-3 modification

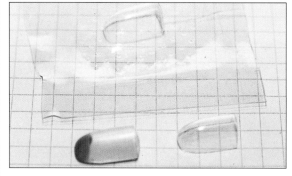

Step 2: The Cowling, Engine and Propeller

You have several options here. Due to the cooling problems with the real Wildcat, a number of cowling, propeller and spinner combinations were tried, so check your references and pick one you like.

For the -2, I selected an early configuration of a 'short' rounded cowling. Since I never throw anything away, I had a spare Airfix SBD cowling (the kit comes with two), and it only took some minor rework to get the shape I was looking for. I filled the SBD gun troughs, removed the kit exhaust stubs and turned the cowling on a Dremel tool to get a consistently rounded profile. The SBD cowl fits very nicely on a sanding attachment making the process relatively easy. An added benefit of this approach is the plastic in the Airfix cowl is so thick, there is still plenty of 'meat' left to mate with the fuselage without extra shims. On this version there is a very obvious raised joint at the 4 and 8 o'clock positions of the cowl. I used a piece of aluminium tape to represent this and sanded the edges to ease the abruptness of the seam. Two 30cal. nose gun troughs and gun blast tubes are also prominent features. Carve or file the troughs into the top of the cowling, and add pieces of 20thou rod or sprue to give the right effect. Add a new carburettor air scoop at the cowl-fuselage joint. The propeller is an Aeroclub Hamilton Standard, 11ft variable pitch unit, trimmed to a scale 10ft.

For the -3, the shape of the stock Hasegawa cowl looks okay. Again, check your references as some photos show a carburettor air scoop in the nose and others do not. I chose the version without the scoop. To salvage my Airfix cowling, I made a resin cast of the Hasegawa Martlet cowl ring and used filler to bring the shape back into a more circular cross section. After filling the kit cowl flap lines, I cut holes on either side of the cowl and made new, single, cowl flaps from the increasingly popular beverage can aluminium. These were attached in the open position to provide a little variation in the profile. My prop came from the spares box, as did the large spinner. The blades were cut and shaped to the proper 9ft diameter and do not have cuffs, although these were added on the prototype at some time during development.

The Pratt & Whitney R-1830 engines for both the -2 and -3 came from a spares box Revell PBY. I removed the plastic blobs that were supposed to be magnetos and added smaller renditions made from scrap. This is not necessary if you are using the Hasegawa kit, but first aid is definitely needed for the Airfix and Frog/Academy kits. (In retrospect, I wish I had used some cast copies of the Hasegawa engine as they are much better). Shown from top to bottom are RTV moulds I made from the Hasegawa originals, the Hasegawa P&W R-1830 and Martlet cowl ring and the resin copies. I used these to upgrade my Frog and Revell kits.) The exhaust stubs are very prominent on both versions and were made from 90thou aluminium tubing. On the -2 they come straight down at the rear of the cowl, whereas the -3's are slightly more recessed and angled to the rear.

Step 3: Wings

This portion of the operation is not too radical, but it is still very distinctive. Before the Wildcat was optimised for mass production, the wingtips were rounded as shown in Figure 6. This is in addition to a shorter span of 34ft on the -2 vs. 38ft in the -3 and production versions. Cut and shape the wing to the rounded tip -2 and remove all surface detail, filling any panel and aileron lines. Re-scribe the longer span ailerons for the respective version, and add the fabric rib treatment described elsewhere. Re-scribe the flap joint, and add 5thou styrene strips for hinges. There was a very pronounced channel or ridge running chord-wise just inboard of the ailerons on the -2 only, which I added using some 5thou styrene strips. Remove the oil coolers for the -2 and replace them with an aluminium scoop on the port wing only. My references mention provision for 50cal. guns in the wings, but I could detect no evidence of any ports, panels or ejector chutes in the photos, so I omitted them entirely. I added scribed lines above and below each wing over the spar/skin joint.

Step 4: Landing Gear and Canopy Details

Before adding the landing gear, mark a semicircular line on bulkhead # at the limits of the kit's wheel cut-out. Using a Dremel or similar routing tool, carve out the wheel indentations. The double thickness of the bulkheads should provide more than ample material for this procedure. A short keel section was also added along the bottom of the wheel well opening.

The landing gear from the Airfix kit is too basic to use as is. As far as I can tell, the landing gear on the real Wildcat did not change at all throughout the production run, so any kit version will work if you are happy with the level of detail. I scratchbuilt mine from plastic and brass rod and tubing shamelessly using the Hasegawa kit as a guide.

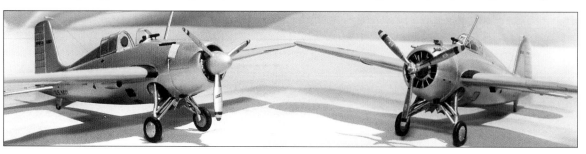

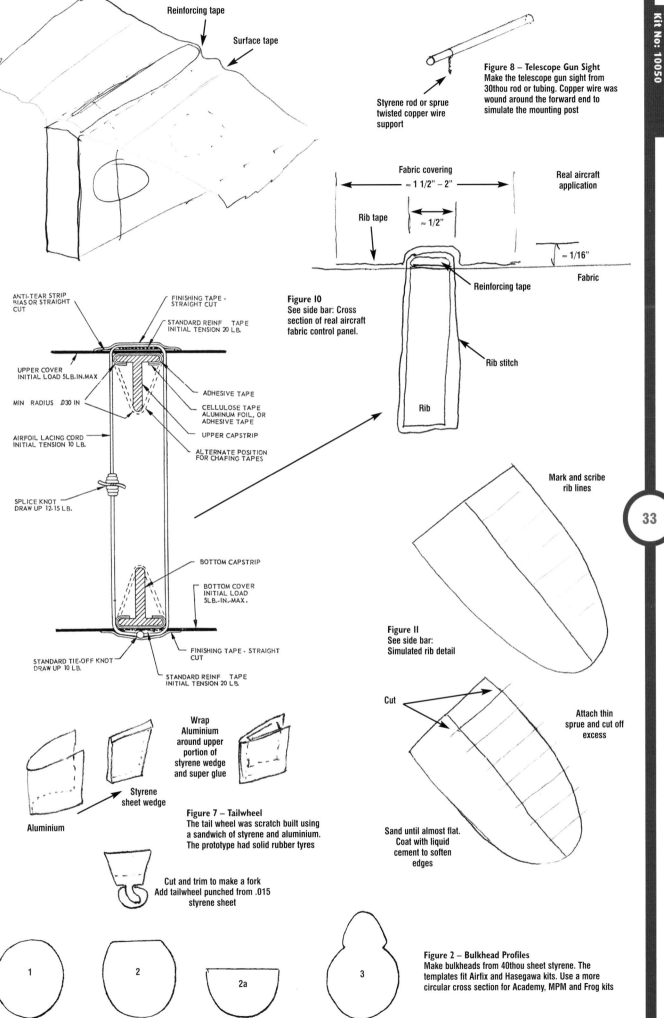

Reinforcing tape

Surface tape

Figure 8 – Telescope Gun Sight
Make the telescope gun sight from
30thou rod or tubing. Copper wire was
wound around the forward end to
simulate the mounting post

Styrene rod or sprue
twisted copper wire
support

Fabric covering
≈ 1 1/2" – 2"

Real aircraft
application

Rib tape

≈ 1/2"

≈ 1/16"

Fabric

Reinforcing tape

Figure 10
See side bar: Cross
section of real aircraft
fabric control panel.

Rib stitch

Rib

ANTI-TEAR STRIP
BIAS OR STRAIGHT
CUT

FINISHING TAPE -
STRAIGHT CUT

STANDARD REINF. TAPE
INITIAL TENSION 20 LB.

UPPER COVER
INITIAL LOAD 5LB.IN.MAX.

ADHESIVE TAPE

MIN RADIUS .030 IN

CELLULOSE TAPE
ALUMINUM FOIL, OR
ADHESIVE TAPE

AIRFOIL LACING CORD
INITIAL TENSION 10 LB.

UPPER CAPSTRIP

ALTERNATE POSITION
FOR CHAFING TAPES

SPLICE KNOT
DRAW UP 12-15 LB.

BOTTOM CAPSTRIP

BOTTOM COVER
INITIAL LOAD
5LB.-IN.-MAX.

STANDARD TIE-OFF KNOT
DRAW UP 10 LB.

FINISHING TAPE - STRAIGHT
CUT

STANDARD REINF. TAPE
INITIAL TENSION 20 LB.

Mark and scribe
rib lines

Figure 11
See side bar:
Simulated rib detail

Cut

Attach thin
sprue and cut off
excess

Sand until almost flat.
Coat with liquid
cement to soften
edges

Wrap
Aluminium
around upper
portion of
styrene wedge
and super glue

Styrene
sheet wedge

Aluminium

Figure 7 – Tailwheel
The tail wheel was scratch built using
a sandwich of styrene and aluminium.
The prototype had solid rubber tyres

Cut and trim to make a fork
Add tailwheel punched from .015
styrene sheet

1   2   2a   3

Figure 2 – Bulkhead Profiles
Make bulkheads from 40thou sheet styrene. The
templates fit Airfix and Hasegawa kits. Use a more
circular cross section for Academy, MPM and Frog kits

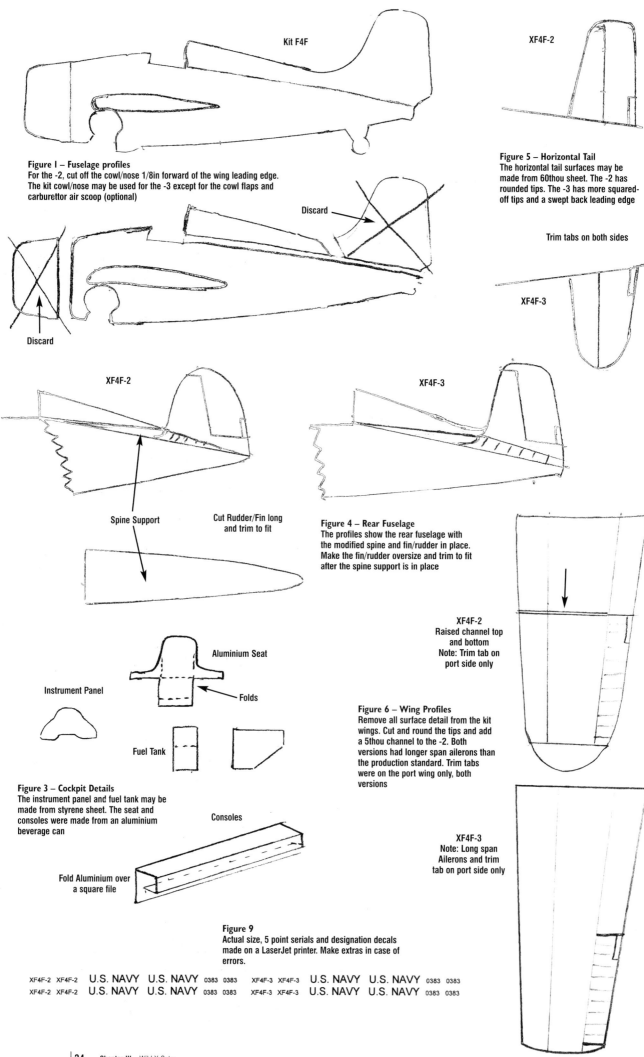

Kit F4F

Figure I – Fuselage profiles
For the -2, cut off the cowl/nose 1/8in forward of the wing leading edge.
The kit cowl/nose may be used for the -3 except for the cowl flaps and
carburettor air scoop (optional)

Discard

Discard

XF4F-2

XF4F-3

Spine Support

Cut Rudder/Fin long
and trim to fit

Aluminium Seat

Instrument Panel

Folds

Fuel Tank

Figure 3 – Cockpit Details
The instrument panel and fuel tank may be
made from styrene sheet. The seat and
consoles were made from an aluminium
beverage can

Consoles

Fold Aluminium over
a square file

Figure 9
Actual size, 5 point serials and designation decals
made on a LaserJet printer. Make extras in case of
errors.

| XF4F-2 XF4F-2 | U.S. NAVY U.S. NAVY | 0383 0383 | XF4F-3 XF4F-3 | U.S. NAVY U.S. NAVY | 0383 0383 |
| XF4F-2 XF4F-2 | U.S. NAVY U.S. NAVY | 0383 0383 | XF4F-3 XF4F-3 | U.S. NAVY U.S. NAVY | 0383 0383 |

XF4F-2

Figure 5 – Horizontal Tail
The horizontal tail surfaces may be
made from 60thou sheet. The -2 has
rounded tips. The -3 has more squared-
off tips and a swept back leading edge

Trim tabs on both sides

XF4F-3

Figure 4 – Rear Fuselage
The profiles show the rear fuselage with
the modified spine and fin/rudder in place.
Make the fin/rudder oversize and trim to fit
after the spine support is in place

XF4F-2
Raised channel top
and bottom
Note: Trim tab on
port side only

Figure 6 – Wing Profiles
Remove all surface detail from the kit
wings. Cut and round the tips and add
a 5thou channel to the -2. Both
versions had longer span ailerons than
the production standard. Trim tabs
were on the port wing only, both
versions

XF4F-3
Note: Long span
Ailerons and trim
tab on port side only

The ubiquitous beverage can provided the material for the gear doors. Refrain from the temptation to box off the gear wells, the real Wildcat was wide open from side to side.

The tailwheel on the prototype was a small, solid rubber type. I constructed a new tailwheel from a sandwich of thin styrene sheet and can aluminium. The tailwheel itself was made using a circular disc and 15thou sheet.

The canopy is different from the production models. Not surprisingly, it seems there are several options here also. Neither the -2 nor -3 had the bulletproof face plate. The -2 had a V-shaped, flat plate windscreen, (See Photo 21) and the -3's was more rounded in the windscreen area. I could not find a suitable substitute, so I vac-formed new ones. I made a new mould, using the kit supplied canopy as a basis. I added filler to the windscreen area to build it up to the desired shape. The modified canopy mould was then filled with plaster to prevent distortion from the hot clear sheet during the vac-forming process. By using the kit part as the basis, you avoid any contour mating problems with the spine. Make sure to remove the kit frame lines by sanding and blending the filler well; any blemishes will show up on the new canopy. I used the plastic vac-formed packaging material from razor blades, flashlight battery, or similar item packages. This plastic is thin, readily available and often clear enough to use for small canopy applications. Plan to make several copies if you want to show off your cockpit details by having the canopy open. It is also nice to have a spare in case you damage the canopy while trimming it to fit. I made three of each version and used every one of them!

Add an antenna mast forward and to the left of the cockpit. The -2 mast is vertical but leans to the left, while the -3 leans left and forward. Both versions had a telescope gun sight. I used a section of 30thou rod and made the mount of thin copper wire (Figure 8).

Step 5: Final Finishing & Colour Scheme

Testors Model Master Enamels were used exclusively. Due to all the sanding and filling, special care should be taken with a primer coat to catch the inevitable scratches and imperfections. Regular grey primer (Testors #2737) was used for the fuselage and lower wings, but I used flat white (#1768) to help brighten the final yellow coat on the upper surface of the wings. The standard US Navy colour scheme of the day was Aluminum (#1781) paint overall, except for the top surface of the wing which was chrome yellow (#1707, FS.13538).

A word of caution is needed here. Reference photos of the -2 clearly show the colour demarcation at the leading edge. Although a directive which prescribed the method of wrapping the yellow around the leading edge (5% of chord) was not published until 1940, some biplanes of the period, as well as the -3, were painted accordingly. Perhaps the directive validated what was becoming a common practice. In any event, it is another little detail that makes the models unique. All interior surfaces were also painted aluminium except for the consoles, glare shield and instrument panel, which are flat black (#1749).

Decals for the national markings were taken from Superscale sheet

72-668 and are the pre-war white star/red centre on blue in four wing positions. The black US NAVY came from the same sheet. The Bureau Number, 0383 for both the -2 and -3, and the model designations, XF4F-2 and XF4F-3, presented a problem. I did not have anything small enough for the model, so I used my word processor and LaserJet printer to print out small 5 point letters on a sheet of clear decal paper (Figure 9). Although the font was not perfect and the black not as intense as a decal, I thought it was close enough for my old eyes. As a precaution, I coated them with liquid decal film before application, and it worked great! Clear Testors Glosscote Lacquer was airbrushed overall before and after the decals were applied. Wing walks should be flat black. The miscellaneous hand-holds, ports and accents were made from black decal sheet or hand painted. The propeller markings came from the spares box for the -2, but I used my imagination for the -3. Some dabs of yellow and blue paint on a stripe of red decal did the trick. I have no idea if the colours are correct, but they add a nice touch.

The propeller tips are marked in accordance with the then current regulations with 4in stripes of Insignia Red (FS.11136), Orange Yellow (FS.13538) and Insignia Blue (FS.15044), with red being the outermost colour. Close inspection of the photographs in my references show another anomaly in that the rear faces of the propeller blades were not painted black as was the usual custom (and regulation). After attaching the canopies, the final details of hypodermic needle pitot tubes and 'invisible' nylon thread antenna wire were added. Other than some oil smears on the bellies, I would recommend weathering sparingly or not at all. I suspect these Wildcats were pampered kittens.

References

• *Aero Detail 22: F4F Wildcat* by Shigeru Nahara, Tommo Yamada & Masato Tanaka, ©1998.
• *Air Enthusiast No.68, Corpulent Feline* by Ken Wixley, Key Publishing, Ltd., ©1997.
• *Detail & Scale Vol.65: F4F Wildcat* by Bert Kinzey, Squadron/Signal Publications, Inc., ©2000.
• *F4F Wildcat In Action, No.1084* by Don Linn, Squadron/Signal Publications, Inc., ©1998.
• *Grumman F4F Wildcat, Warpaint Series No.9* by Glenn Phillips, Hall Park Books, Ltd., ©1997.

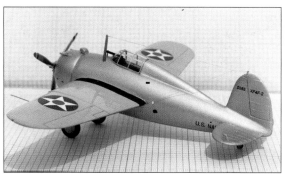

Chapter IV

BOEING 737
Scale: 1/144
Kit No: 01478
Type: Injection Moulded Plastic
Manufacturer: Airfix

Airfix Kit 01478

The Captain and the Dirty Vicar

The Boeing 737 my father flew - in three different airline liveries!

By John Stokes

Where does your inspiration to model a particular subject come from? Sometimes it just creeps up on you unexpectedly, and before you know it a plan is forming in your mind. So it was in a conversation with my father, who had been fortunate enough to spend his career flying a number of different aircraft types. One such was the Boeing 737-200 series, which he first encountered in British Airways service.

One particular aircraft, G-DDDV, was informally referred to as the 'Dirty Vicar' rather than by its correct phonetic callsign of 'Delta Victor'. A number of hours were logged on 'DV before he delivered it to Gatwick for transfer to the British Airtours division of BA. No more was seen of her before early retirement beckoned, and the life of leisure that should have followed.

Researching this aircraft threw light on how a modern airliner can be used and traded around various airlines. Manufacturer's serial number 22633 first flew on the 2 March 1981 and was delivered to Air Europe seventeen days later. After eighteen months the aircraft was leased to Air Florida for two years, before going to British

Airways at the end of 1984. Four years with BA was followed by service with GB Airways before a return to Air Europe. At the end of 1989 it left the British Register and became A40-BL with Gulf Air, staying until 1993. A succession of South American owners then followed, until joining Southern Winds in Argentina in 2003 as LV-YGB.

It seemed to me that the 'Dirty Vicar' in three liveries would make an interesting line-up of models. A look through my airliner collection revealed only two Airfix 737s, but a quick call to those helpful folk at The Aviation Hobby Shop saw another one through the letterbox in a few days.

The kit was first issued in the late 1960s and is fairly basic with few parts. It comes with the British Airways 'Landor' scheme, so I had been keeping an eye out for decal sheets for the Air Europe and Gulf Air schemes. Air Europe's turned up on Hannants' website and the Gulf Air one I found while browsing at the IPMS Nationals. I also found a couple of 737 window decal sheets produced by Airline Hobby Supplies, so now had everything I needed to make a start on modelling the career of the 'Dirty Vicar'.

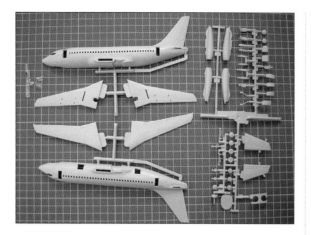

First issued in the 1960s, the kit is basic by modern standards

Three different releases of the Airfix B737 that John used for his models

Aftermarket Air Europe and Gulf Air and the Airfix kit's British Airways decals

Cabin doors installed slightly proud of the surface to facilitate sanding flush later

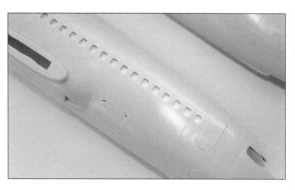

Plasticard strip cemented behind the cabin windows, which would be filled and sanded flush

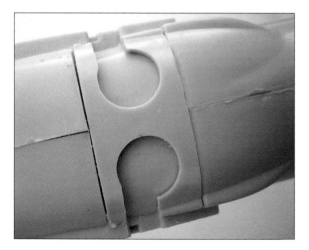

Kit provides just shallow recesses for the main landing gear bays

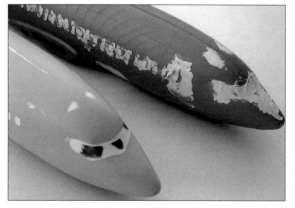

Cabin window apertures and cockpit windscreen filled with Milliput and sanded flush

37

Cabin window apertures and cockpit windscreen filled with Milliput and sanded flush

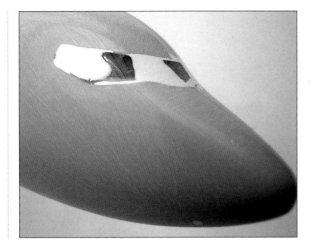

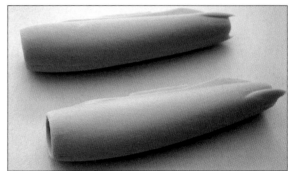

Completed fuselages sprayed with Halfords Appliance White gloss

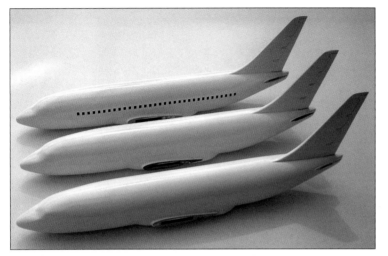

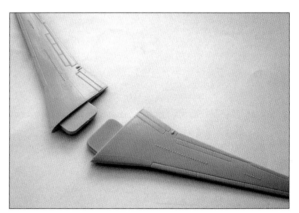

Wings and engine nacelle⁰s required filling and sanding

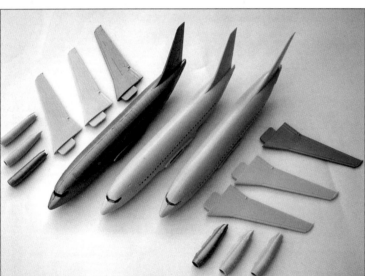

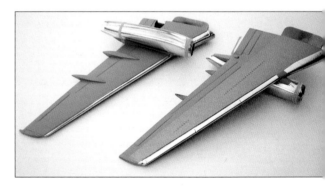

Completed sub-assemblies for all three models

Alclad Chrome reproduces polished engine nacelles well, while different metallic shades further enhance realistic appearance

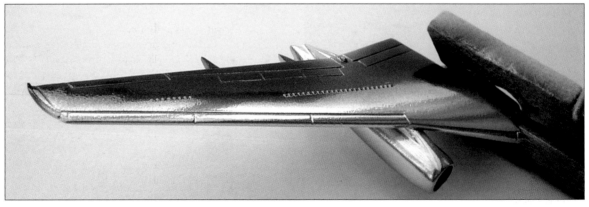

Trial-fitting wings revealed "wobbly and indistinct fit"

John retained the kit's window openings for his British Airways model, applying matt black paint around the frames before filling with Clearfix to create the impression of flush-fitting windows

Fuselage

I had no intention of producing three superdetailed B737s, just a set of neatly built models. It doesn't take long to put all the main components together, so I did all three models in one period of basic construction, but will mainly describe just one here.

The doors and cargo hold hatches were cemented in, but note that the rear doors numbered 2 and 3 should be swapped over, as the instructions have got them reversed and neither will fit otherwise. I pushed them out from the inside so that they stood slightly proud of the fuselage to make it easier to sand them flush afterwards. If you don't do this they sit slightly recessed and require building up with filler to get a flush finish. Showing my age, I went to get the strips of windows out of the box and cement them in place. I was going to fill the window openings anyway, but wanted to use them to support the filler, but there they were… gone! Airfix no longer supply the window strips we all used to know and love as kids, so I resorted to using strips of 10-thou plasticard cemented behind the windows to support the filler that would later be pushed in from the outside. As I only had two sets of window decals I left one of the fuselages with its window openings untouched, to fill later with Kristal Kleer or Clearfix.

I intended to use the windshield glass if possible, and so painted the interior of the cockpit and rear bulkhead matt black. To ensure that the finished model stood on all three undercarriage legs rather becoming a tailsitter I stuck a couple of foreign coins to the rear of the cockpit bulkhead — a good use for all that holiday cash not worth changing at the bank! Both halves of the fuselage were now brought together and left overnight to dry.

The fit was not spectacular and required some work with wet 'n' dry paper to tidy it up. At this point I trial-fitted the windshield and immediately abandoned my plans for masking and retaining the clear sections. The fit was very approximate, probably down to the

Polished metal windscreen frame from Airline Hobby Supplies decals required precise positioning

moulds having been well used and becoming worn over the last 30 or so years. On to Plan B then, which was to glue the windshield and apply a liberal coating of Milliput. There were also a few sink marks to be filled, most noticeably just above the windshield. The aftermarket decal sheets provided black windshield decals, so these were going to have to do. I think cabin windows are definitely better as decals, but prefer to have cockpit windows in clear plastic. Because of their larger surface, cockpit window decals are more obvious, but in this case were 100 times better than what the kit offered.

The main wheel bay between the wings comes as a separate part that needs to be fitted at this stage. I say wheel bay, but it's just a shallow impression. I decided I could live with it, but this is one area to which superdetailers would probably want to pay some attention. Once all this was dried a major batch of Milliput Superfine white filler was mixed up to deal with all the fuselages. Two of them had all their side windows filled, and all three had their main fuselage join seams and the area around the main undercarriage bay filled.

All the filler was gradually sanded back and the shape of the cockpit glazing reinstated in solid form using a strip of fine wet 'n' dry paper secured to a small piece of Aeroclub's Tee-Al. This allowed me to sand the windshield while keeping a flat surface and the correct angles. By now a lot of the raised panel lines were disappearing, but that was fine by me. In this scale I don't think that panel lines are either desirable or necessary. From a scale viewing distance they simply wouldn't be visible on a real aircraft, and any difference between panels is better depicted by tonal variations in paint.

With the fuselages smoothed and sanded down it looked like all the windows and doors were neatly blended in, so I applied a couple of coats of Halfords white primer. This showed that the window areas in particular were not as neat as I had imagined, so further sanding and filling were necessary. Once lightly rubbed down again, a couple of coats of Halfords gloss appliance white followed.

Wings, Engines and Tailplane

I assembled the wings and engines, but kept them separate until after filling and sanding down. Ideally I would have kept them like this until after painting, but test fitting showed that the fit of engines to wings was going to leave gaps. Rather than having to fill and patch after painting I glued the engines in place and saw to any filling before painting started. It was going to make masking a bit more fiddly, but the final finish would be better. I sanded all the raised panel lines off the wings and engines, which were covered with them. The 737-200 has very smooth engine cowlings, so it is worth taking off all the clunky looking detail. Once glued to the wings the gap between the two pieces was very apparent. One point to note is that

39

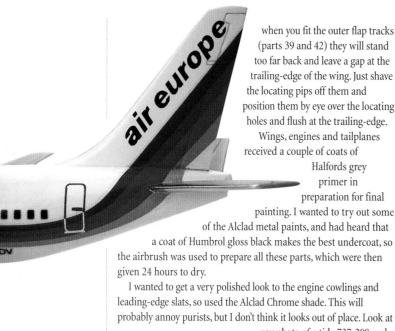

when you fit the outer flap tracks (parts 39 and 42) they will stand too far back and leave a gap at the trailing-edge of the wing. Just shave the locating pips off them and position them by eye over the locating holes and flush at the trailing-edge.

Wings, engines and tailplanes received a couple of coats of Halfords grey primer in preparation for final painting. I wanted to try out some of the Alclad metal paints, and had heard that a coat of Humbrol gloss black makes the best undercoat, so the airbrush was used to prepare all these parts, which were then given 24 hours to dry.

I wanted to get a very polished look to the engine cowlings and leading-edge slats, so used the Alclad Chrome shade. This will probably annoy purists, but I don't think it looks out of place. Look at any photo of a tidy 737-200 and most of them have a mirror-like finish on their highly polished cowlings.

Following the Alclad instructions closely and misting on a few coats I have to say the results were stunning. These are certainly well polished engine cowlings! Not only does the finish look good, but also it has proved very durable. I masked off the cowlings and leading-edge slats with a mix of Tamiya and normal masking tape, and airbrushed a coat of light grey over the rest of the wings. Once this was dry the flaps and trailing-edges were masked off and the wing box centre-section sprayed. I mixed my own brand of 'Corroguard' for this job, about 50/50 Humbrol 67 tank grey and Metalcote 27002 silver, which gives just the right tone of medium silver-grey for this elusive colour. A little further masking was done on the cowlings to brush paint slightly different tones of silver on the intake lips and thrust reverser buckets.

Trial-fitting the wings revealed a very wobbly and indistinct fit. Sanding and scraping the wing roots firmed up the fit, which varied on all three models. The worst of them had a very noticeable gap, but at least all was square and with the correct dihedral. The gaps were filled with a 50/50 mix of white glue and water. When dry a thin brush coat of Tamiya acrylic white improved the appearance.

Decalling British Airways

You may have already looked at the pictures accompanying this article, and thought 'That's odd, it doesn't look like a BA scheme?' Well, quite right, it is an odd scheme. G-DDDV started life with Air Europe and had an overall white fuselage. On moving to British Airways it received an interim scheme, presumably to get it into

Combination of paint and kit decals was used to reproduce the 'Dirty Vicar's' hybrid BA scheme

service as quickly as possible. As it later returned to Air Europe I assume it was probably leased and I am not sure if it ever received the full BA 'Landor' livery with the lower fuselage in dark blue and the upper in that strange shade of silvery white.

The Airfix kit comes with decals for the full Landor livery, which was only partly useful. I couldn't use the fin markings as they included the heraldic crest and 'last two' of the registration 'YF'. It was simple enough to mask and spray the blue areas using Humbrol 15 lightened with a touch of white. I cut the red stripes from the kit decals and used those. This model was the one retaining the kit windows, which were later going to be filled with Humbrol Clearfix. A tip here is to take a fine brush and paint matt black around the insides of the windows. Wipe any excess off with some white spirit on a cloth. It helps to create the illusion of the finished window being flush with the outside of the fuselage.

The cockpit window decals came from an Airline Hobby Supplies sheet, with the black going on first followed by the silver edging when it was dry. It takes a lot of checking from all angles, but is absolutely critical to get right. Next up were the door outlines from an old Microscale sheet. The British Airways titles came from the kit. I had previously masked and brush-painted the bare metal leading-edge to the fin on all three models.

I really like this colour scheme and think it is much cleaner and smarter than the full Landor scheme. It's a shame that BA didn't adopt it across the whole fleet!

Air Europe

I used the side window decals from the Airline Hobby Supplies sheet and put them on first so that I could line up all subsequent decals on them. I had to cut three windows from the port strip and two from the starboard, as they were otherwise too long. The cockpit window decal was provided on the main sheet, which is from Runway 30 (and was why I had a spare to use on the BA model). With these basics done, it was time to move on to those big fuselage stripes, which come in three sections, forward fuselage, rear fuselage, and fin. The instructions advise starting with the rear fuselage section, as the other two line up on it. I started with the port side rear and it went on well enough, but when I put the forward section on I hit a problem. The main stripe contains four stripes within it, going from red through orange to yellow. The trouble was that where the front and rear sections met in the middle they just did not align, so much so that the bottom yellow stripe on the rear section met up with nothing on the forward section. Having to make a quick decision, I lined them up along the top edge as this was going to be most noticeable, and left sorting the problem out until everything had dried. I was bit annoyed with myself for not having checked this first, but then again you don't really expect to have to with aftermarket decals, do you? Of

Captain speaking

I first made the acquaintance of the 'Dirty Vicar' whilst employed by British Airways as a captain on the B737 fleet. She (I understand the clergy are now allowed to be female) was showing her age even then, having had a strenuous career and being much overworked, so much so that she refused to fly straight without much fiddling with the trim wheels, and at one time was continually being 'snagged' for being heavy on the ailerons. This was rectified after a major overhaul when an aileron cable to its relevant hydraulic jack was discovered to be off one of its guide pulleys.

In common with her siblings she could turn around and bite if not handled with some care. For instance, if rotated too enthusiastically on take-off (three degrees per second recommended) she could perform what was described as a 'pitch-up and roll-off', which was just that. When the control column was neutralised on reaching the right attitude, rotation could continue all on its own until a wing dropped. Not nice at any time, let alone close to the ground.

In spite of being fat and ugly, she was quite difficult to slow down even with the use of speedbrakes, and many a driver has been caught out too hot and high on approach. This was partly due to the fact that the engine idle rpm had to be set on the high side in order to meet the minimum acceleration time in the case of an aborted approach.

Once on the ground with reverse thrust deployed one was committed to staying there, as the manufacturer would not guarantee that the reverser buckets would retract due to air loads. But enough of horror stories and on with the saga of the 'Dirty Vicar'.

I retired from BA at the end of 1986 and had twiddled my thumbs for a few months when one day the phone rang, and a voice at the other end asked if I would like a summer job as captain on B737s based in Manchester with an airline called Air Europe? It did not take much to convince me that this could be fun, so I readily accepted. A brief groundschool course was followed by a trip to Liverpool Airport for base flying (circuits and bumps). On arriving I sought out my training captain and we walked out onto the tarmac, where much to my amazement stood G-DDDV gleaming in her new paint scheme. We were soon on good terms again and had many trips together over the summer transporting the bucket-and-spade crowd to their respective beaches. It was on one of these trips to the Greek Islands that I made the acquaintance of the first female co-pilot I had flown with. We parked the aircraft on a patch of concrete very close to a small beach and there, standing on the sand was a nicely tanned

young man waving at us. Fine, but he was wearing precisely…nothing. 'Right, Dave,' says Camilla (for that was her name), 'You now have a mutiny in your hands. I'll be back in an hour!'

After the 1987 summer season was over I was asked to stay on permanently and convert on to the 737-300/400-series aircraft and be based in Gatwick. This suited me fine, as I live about an hour's travelling time from there. Then, in 1991, Air Europe went bust. End of story I thought. But no. After a few months of cooling my heels the phone rang once again and as a result I found myself in Bahrain with Gulf-Air. The plot was to convert back to the B737-200 series (one of the most difficult courses I have ever done, changing from a glass cockpit back to a steam-driven one!). At any rate I once again found myself in charge and flying as far as Athens in the west to Karachi in the east.

Fairly soon after arriving I decided to take my family with me to Dubai, where we had a two-day layover. The aircraft allocated was A40-BL. Somewhere enroute I was doing an instrument scan when my eyes lit on a small metal plate upon which were engraved the letters G-DDDV. Unbelievable! Here she was again. I sometimes wonder if this is a record, to fly the same aircraft in three different liveries?

I finally retired from flying in 1992 when my license expired, but I understand on the best authority that at the time of writing the 'Dirty Vicar' was still soldiering on, this time in Argentina.

41

---

course, I checked the starboard sides before dipping them in water and they were not half as bad. There were slight gaps in the decals, particularly at the base of the fin, and it would have been nice to have a bit of spare stripe to patch things, but there wasn't any, so I had to resort to mixing paints to the best match I could. The red outlines for the doors had unfortunately bled into the carrier film, which if used as it was would have given the doors a pink tint. I carefully cut the

carrier film away from the doors, and applied just the red outline.

The anti-glare panel is supplied as a decal, but I found that it was not quite long enough, so painted in the shortfall once it had dried. With the 'Air Europe' titling on the fuselage and fin, the model was starting to look good.

Gulf Air

This is a very nice sheet produced by ATP, with very realistic gold areas for the titling and falcon on the fin. Some Gulf Air 737s have a bare metal strip on the very lower fuselage, starting behind the nosewheel extending to the rear, and some are all white. I went with the all white option for much the same reasons as with the British Airways model. I would be very surprised if DV had been stripped back upon entering service with Gulf Air.

The side windows were applied from another Airline Hobby Supplies sheet, along with the cockpit area. These have to be applied first so that the triple stripe decal that extends from nose to wing roots can be applied accurately. There is one large decal per side, consisting of all three stripes. Before cutting them from the sheet I noticed that the red stripe was a little too close to the green one on both side decals. All three stripes should be equally spaced, so I carefully cut the red ones free to allow me to position them more

ATP's complex Gulf Air decals conformed well around nose contours

accurately. I applied the port side first and left it overnight to dry. It has to conform to the compound curves of the nose area, and there is plenty of excess decal there. Next day I trimmed the excess back, and applied MicroSol to settle it all back down. Once this was dry, the starboard side was applied in the same way, getting everything lined up. It was worth cutting the red sections free, as I was able to space them with the same separation as between the maroon and green stripes. A nice touch from ATP is that they supply three blocks of the stripe colours on the decal sheet so that you can cut out what you need for any necessary patching. These decals were good, very good, and a pleasure to use.

In Gulf Air service G-DDDV was re-registered A40-BL. The ATP sheet comes with options for the original Gulf Air B737 fleet of A40-BC to -BK. It was a simple matter of trimming the 'Es' to create the required 'L'. (A40-BK disappeared in mysterious circumstances over the Arabian Desert as the result of a terrorist bomb. Presumably 'BL was brought in as a replacement.)

Registration lettering

The BA and Air Europe aircraft both needed registrations on the fuselage sides and under the wings, with the 'last two' each side of the fin and nose gear doors. This was a lot of 'D' letters required, and a

search though my sheets of old decals didn't produce any, never mind the twenty or so I would actually need. I therefore decided to have a go at producing my own on the PC using paper from The Decal Paper Store. The printing was not as sharp as I would have liked, having a faintly blurred edge, but was still usable. Being on continual film each registration had to be cut out, and then soaked. Unfortunately the black ink took on more of a dark purple hue, I assume from being soaked in water, so they weren't really a success. I have left them on the BA and Air Europe models but will replace them as and when I can find something better.

The underwing registrations were even less successful. At first I thought the decals were silvering, so I painted some Johnsons Kleer over them, which seemed to solve the problem. However, I soon realised that the backing paper, although clear when wet, dried white. This was OK on the white fuselages, but not what was wanted on grey wings! I lifted the underwing decals with tape and started again. A good hunt through my decal bank (never throw anything away), produced three old BA Trident sheets with G-ARPD and one VC10 sheet with G-ARVH. Just what I needed, although the 'Vs' were a tad smaller than the other letters. What a shame the small fuselage letters on these sheets were all in white, to go on the blue areas of the standard BA livery. What we need is for one of the decal

manufacturers to produce sheets of civil letters, in the same way as many of them produce sheets for military serials.

Final approach

Three complete sets of undercarriages were assembled and painted, and then installed on each aircraft. The main gear tended to splay outward, so it was essential to check and adjust each one by sighting from head on. The nose gear doors were much too thick, so I replaced them with others cut from 10-thou Plasticard. I would have replaced the main gear doors as well, but they are a very convoluted shape. As they are tucked away underneath and virtually hidden by the engine cowlings, I used them as they were. There area a couple of blade aerials on the fuselage, mounted ventrally and dorsally, which were cut from 5-thou Plasticard and attached with white glue. Finally, a couple of coats of Johnson's Klear was brushed on each model, and my B737 'fleet' was complete.

This was a 'fun' project rather than a serious attempt at highly detailed models. There was an awful lot of filling and sanding to be done, particularly as I had to do everything three times. I am reasonably pleased with the results, but the Airfix kit really does show its age when compared with some more recent airliner kits.

The Airfix decal sheet was pretty good, although I only used a few pieces on each model. The Runway 30 sheet with the Air Europe scheme was a bit of a disappointment in the way that the fuselage stripes were so misaligned. I have since noticed a faint 'bleeding' of red into the carrier film on them. If I were to do this one again I would trim all the carrier film off, and slit along the fuselage stripes where they join, to give some room for adjustment. The ATP decals for the Gulf Air Scheme were excellent, settling down perfectly and with the carrier film completely disappearing.

There are six more liveries to model on 'DV' to show the full set it has worn, but I think I'll stop at this point!

43

Chapter V

KAMAN SH-2F SEASPRITE
Scale: 1/72
Kit No: 03041
Type: Injection Moulded Plastic
Manufacturer: Airfix

Airfix Kit 03041

Seasprite Conversion

Backdating the Airfix SH-2F to a single-engined UH-2B

By Will Alcott

Kaman UH-2B Seasprite BuNo 151310 assigned to the Naval Air Station Jacksonville, Florida, in 1968

Introduction

The Kaman Seasprite was the standard US Navy plane guard (shipboard search and rescue) helicopter throughout the 1960s. It went on to see extensive service in the anti-submarine warfare role, eventually retiring from US service after more than 30 years. Upgraded SH-2G models serve today with the naval air arms of New Zealand, Egypt and Poland.

The first Seasprites were equipped with a single General Electric T58 turboshaft engine. When the single-engined UH-2As and UH-2Bs were pressed into service for Combat Search and Rescue (CSAR) in Vietnam, more power was needed to offset the weight of defensive armament and armour. Many early models were rebuilt with twin T58s as UH-2Cs and HH-2C/Ds.

In 1/72, both Airfix and Fujimi issued Seasprite kits. Both kits represent the SH-2F twin-engined anti-submarine warfare version. Airmodel released a very basic vacuform kit of the UH-2A/B (consisting only of two clear plastic fuselage halves). Rotorcraft released a resin conversion set for the UH-2A/B, currently available through A2Zee Models in the UK.

I picked up the Rotorcraft conversion second-hand with the intention of using it with the Fujimi kit. The conversion is intended for the Airfix kit, and some of the parts appear to be based on modified Airfix parts. When I came across a second-hand Airfix kit I was very impressed. The Seasprite was one of Airfix's last releases in the 1980s, and while panel and rivet detail is raised, the kit features a

The main instrument panel as supplied by Airfix will need some modification to depict an earlier single-engined machine, although given the level of clarity through the glazing simply omitting the central scope should suffice

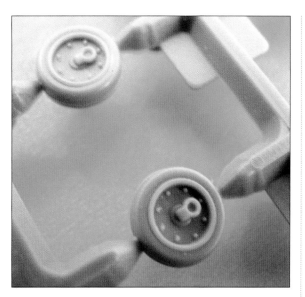

The kit main wheels are good – in fact the overall level of detail throughout was a pleasant surprise

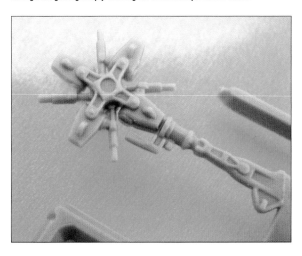

Airfix's rotor hub. The Seasprite was one of the last of what many regard as the 'original' Airfix kits, and is of a comparatively late vintage

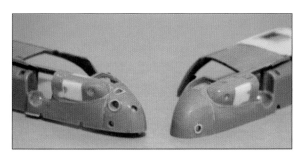

A closer look at the new spotlights and other openings added to the nose

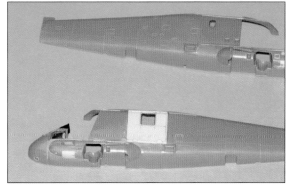

The engine and tail rotor pylon have been removed from the fuselage halves, smoke float boxes removed from sponsons, and the sonobuoy launcher replaced with a cabin door opening. The three-bladed tail rotor has been scratchbuilt

The new sliding door has been added in place of the sonobuoy launcher, sized and located based on Aviation News drawings

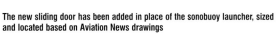

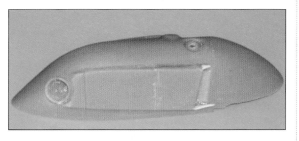

The resin engine hump with intake deepened and lips redefined. The exhaust still requires some correction

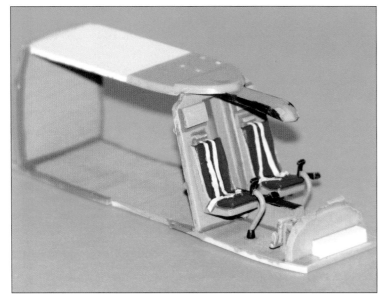

A front view showing the fit of the resin hump. The glazing is typically thick and the moulded wipers unfortunate

The cabin interior with anti-submarine equipment deleted, and new roof section added

Engine, tail rotor pylon and windscreen have now been added

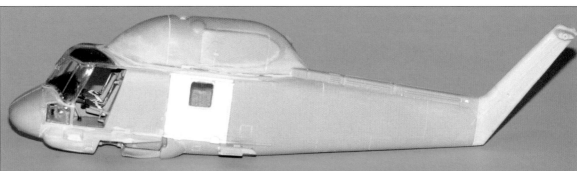

This view of the underside shows the amount of holes filled in to effect the conversion. Despite appearances the model is very nearly ready for painting

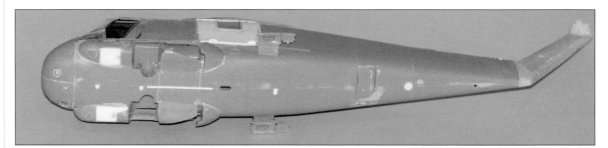

Starboard side view with all the conversion parts now firmly faired in. The exhaust has been drilled out to be replaced with thinned Evergreen tube

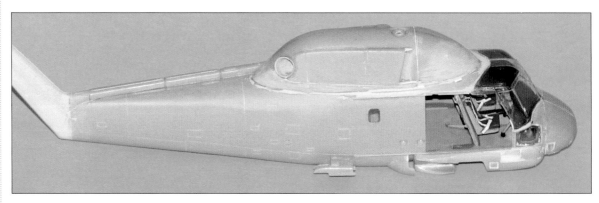

Transparencies masked and new exhaust fitted, the conversion work is pretty much done

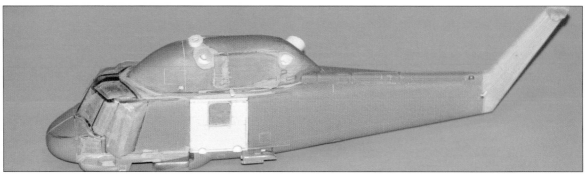

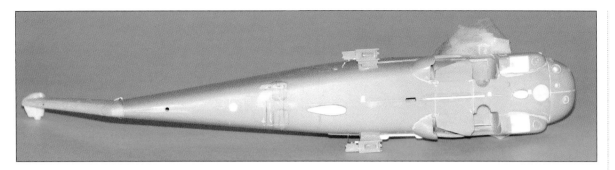

Additional aerials and fairings have been fitted to the underside

well detailed interior, rotor hub and landing gear. I opted to use the Airfix kit for this conversion.

The Rotorcraft conversion includes three cast resin parts and a length of plastic coated wire. The resin parts provide the single engine/transmission hump, a narrow chord tail rotor pylon, and a second external fuel tank, while the wire comes bent to shape for the 'fishing pole' rescue hoist seen on early Seasprites. The set only provides the basics – it's up to the modeller to convert the four-bladed tail rotor to three blades, and to scratchbuild the port aft cabin door. The instruction sheet contains only written directions. Drawings would be useful, particularly for the new cabin door. The best reference source I've found was an Aviation News article from February 1990, which contained drawings of both sides of the fuselage for all major Seasprite variants.

Construction

The Rotorcraft instructions suggest starting by removing the engine section and tail rotor pylon from the fuselage halves of the Airfix kit. With hindsight, I'd recommend leaving the tail rotor pylon in place. To fit the replacement narrow chord pylon you must fill a seam through the middle of the moulded detail at the base of the pylon, but I'd recommend carving the extended chord section away from the kit pylon, avoiding the need to fill any seams.

Airfix provide a reasonably complete anti-submarine interior. With no details available on the interior of the utility versions, I simply omitted the sonar equipment and operator's seat. The instrument panel features decent raised detail, likely correct for a twin-engined Seasprite. Lacking any information on the panel for the single-engined versions, I simply blanked off the large central radar scope. I added a roof to the rear section from sheet styrene, but the only details I added to the interior were some lead foil seatbelts. The cabin interior was painted Dark Gull Gray, with red seat cushions, off-white belts, and black details on the instrument panel and overhead console.

The Airfix kit comes with the sonobuoy launcher moulded on the port fuselage, but utility versions of the Seasprite had a sliding door in this location. After removing the sonobuoy detail, I used the Aviation News drawings to cut a new door from 20-thou sheet

styrene. The cabin window was cut from clear styrene.

I used scrap plastic to fill in the openings for the smoke marker floats in the landing gear sponsons, and almost all the mounting holes for the underside antennae and fairings can be filled as well. The nose of the Seasprite featured several recessed spotlights, so I drilled out holes for each of these. In the interest of being as accurate as possible, I relocated the fuel filler slightly lower and further forward on the starboard side, added the fuel filler cap with a disk of plastic created with a punch and die set, and added a new filler cap to the windshield de-icer tank in the starboard sponson.

At this stage I assembled the fuselage. The parts fit well, although removing the engine/transmission housing made the fuselage halves much more flexible. Given the amount of filling and sanding to come, I decided to remove all raised panel and rivet detail and rescribed steps, access panels, and selected panel lines, using an Olfa P-Cutter.

Installing the resin engine section required a lot of test fitting. I used a Dremel tool to remove excess resin from the undersurface of the engine casting, but the resin engine hump doesn't quite match reference photos. In particular, the intake lacks definition, and the exhaust seems too small. I deepened the intake using a steel cutter in the Dremel, and added small triangles of thin plastic to define the edges of the intake lips. I also used the Dremel to remove the moulded-in exhaust, and replaced it with a larger diameter section of Evergreen tubing with the walls thinned.

The overhead windows and windscreen are provided as a single part in the Airfix kit. They are well moulded, and the fit was good. I filled the mounting points for the rear view mirror on the starboard edge of the windscreen, and after dipping the clear parts in Future/Klear, I sprayed a coat of Tamiya clear green acrylic on the inside of the overhead windows.

The Rotorcraft kit provides a section of bent wire for the rescue hoist, appropriate for early Seasprites. I chose to model an aircraft with the later style of hoist arm that retracted flush into the front of the engine housing, and rather than try to scribe the outline of the hoist arm cover into the compound curve of the engine housing, I drew the shape on 3M Scotch Magic Tape, cut it out and attached it permanently to the engine housing with superglue. The result was a slightly raised hoist cover panel.

47

Yellow areas are masked and painted, and the base Engine Gray lightened with panel shading

The A through C models featured single-wheeled main landing gear struts, whereas later versions had dual wheels. I had no detail references on the single wheel gear, so I simply cut the inner axle from the gear strut, and fitted only the outer wheel to each strut. The tailwheel and strut can be used as is from the Airfix kit; however the strut needs to be moved further aft.

The Seasprite was equipped with two pylons to carry fuel tanks or other stores. The Airfix kit provides a single fuel tank, and the Rotorcraft set provides a second. The Rotorcraft part is the same

SEASPRITE GENERAL CHARACTERISTICS		
Length: 52 ft 2 in (15.90 m)		
Rotor diameter: 44 ft 0 in (13.41 m)		
Height: 13 ft 6 in (4.11 m)		
Disc area: 1520.53 sq ft (141.26 sq m)		
Empty weight: 6,100 lb (2,127 kg)		
Max takeoff weight: 10,200 lb (4,627 kg)		
Powerplant: 1× General Electric T58-GE-8B turboshaft, 1,525 shp (1,137 kW)		
Maximum speed: 141 knots (162 mph, 261 km/h)		
Range: 582 nmi (670 mi, 1,080 km)		
Service ceiling: 17,400 ft (5,305 m)		
Super Seasprite General characteristics		
Crew: 3 (Pilot, Co-pilot/Tactical Coordinator (TACCO), Sensor Operator (SENSO))		
Length: 52 ft 9 in (15.9 m)		
Rotor diameter: 45 ft 0 in (13.4 m)		
Height: 15 ft 0 in (4.5 m)		
Disc area: 44 ft 4 in (13.5 m)		
Empty weight: 9,200 lb (4,170 kg)		
Max takeoff weight: 13,500 lb (6,120 kg)		
Powerplant: 2× T700-GE-401/401C turboshaft, 1,723 shp (1,285 kW) each		
Maximum speed: 138 knots (256 km/h, 159 mph)		
Range: 540 nmi (1,000 km, 869 mi)		
Service ceiling: 18,000 ft (3,000 m)		

ARMAMENT		
Torpedoes: 2× Mk 46 or Mk 50 ASW torpedoes		
Hardpoints: 2× side fuselage mounting stub/pylon stations		
Missiles: Non-US aircraft carry a variety of guided missiles, including the AGM-65 Maverick (often used in the anti-ship role) and dedicated anti-ship missiles		

shape as the Airfix part, but lacks detail, so I added a ring of wire to represent the filler cap, and scribed seams into the resin tank.

The Airfix rotor features good detail, and seems accurate for both single- and twin-engined versions. I simply removed the raised details from the blades. The tail rotor requires more work – the UH-2A through UH-2C models featured a three-bladed tail rotor. I used three of the kit blades with a scratchbuilt hub and pitch-change mechanism.

Small scratchbuilt details included the pitot tube mounted above the port forward door, position lights mounted on stalks above each aft cabin door, two grab handles at the base of the tail rotor pylon, tie-downs on the engine housing and tail-rotor pylon, and the High-Frequency wire aerial running to the port horizontal stabilizer. The lights and pitot were shaped from plastic strip, while I used fuse wire for the grab handles and tie down rings.

I masked the clear parts with a mix of Tamiya tape, 3M Scotch Magic Tape and Bare-Metal Foil, leaving the sliding doors separate, and masked off the interior openings with Tamiya tape.

Painting

Early Seasprites were colourful, featuring large areas of fluorescent red-orange. Utility and anti-submarine versions spent most of their careers in overall gloss Engine Gray (FS16081). The horizontal stabilizers and bracing struts were normally painted in red and yellow stripes.

After a primer coat of Dark Gull Gray, I sprayed the aft fuselage flat white. I applied a coat of Insignia yellow over this, then masked off the relevant areas before applying an initial coat of Engine Gray, but the model looked too dark, so I mixed Engine Gray with about 30% Dark Gull Gray, and using a fine tip on my Paasche H I applied the lightened gray in random patterns, concentrating on the middle sections of each panel. All colours were Model Master enamels.

While the fuselage was drying, I turned to the rotors. The tailrotor blades have white/red/white tips and black blades, and each main rotor blade is flat black both on the underside and on the leading 1/3 of the upper chord, and light gray on the remaining 2/3 of the upper surface, with a natural metal leading edge, and yellow tips. Airfix provide decals for this, however their tones looked off, so I went through the tedious process of masking and spraying each colour.

I sprayed the wheel wells white, along with the main gear struts and mainwheels, then masked and sprayed the black anti-glare panel on the nose. When everything was dry, I sprayed a coat of Humbrol clear gloss in preparation for decals.

Decals

I know of no decals for the utility version of the Seasprite. Eventually I gathered enough references to allow the model to be finished using spares box decals and white US Navy letter/number decals from

above the Bureau number.

Rather than mask and paint the red stripes on the tailplanes and struts, I used Scale-Master Insignia Red decal stripes, while black and white decal stripes were used for the step markings on the fuselage.

I sealed the decals with a second gloss coat, then applied a wash of black watercolour to highlight panel and vent details. On the landing gear struts and wheels I used a Payne's grey wash, and once dry, removed the excess with a damp cloth.

I applied Humbrol Satin Coat for a semi-gloss finish and painted the navigation lights with Tamiya clear acrylics. I then attached the remaining small detail parts and added the HF wire aerial from nylon monofilament, painted flat black, leaving the main rotor separate to avoid damage when transporting the model.

Conclusions

This was a project for which gathering references and deciding which aircraft to build took far longer than actual construction. The Airfix kit is surprisingly good, and builds into an excellent representation of the SH-2F straight from the box. The Rotorcraft kit is fairly easy to use, and I understand recent examples include more detailed instructions regarding the port side cabin door.

Scale-Master. I chose to depict a UH-2B of Helicopter Combat Support Squadron 1 (HC-1), aboard the *USS Kitty Hawk* during 1966-1967. An unusual feature of the markings was the presentation of the carrier name on the sides of the engine housing, with the letters USS KITTY arrayed in an arc above HAWK.

Creating the unique markings was just a slow process of applying individual letter/number decals. The Scale-Master sheet includes *USS Kitty Hawk* titles, which I cut apart and applied as nine separate decals. I used the Airfix tailrotor warning markings, cut apart and rearranged, and national insignia came from Superscale. The only markings I omitted were the tiny UH-2B letters that should appear

References
- *Aviation News*, 2-15 February 1990
- *Orphans of the 7th Fleet* by Mark Morgan

49

The Light Fantastic

Kaman's busy Seasprite

By Paul Stapleton

Development and Introduction

When the US Navy identified a need for a fast all-weather multi-role rotary aircraft in the late 1950s, the winning design to emerge from the competition was Kaman's model K-20, resulting in a contract for four prototype and twelve production HU2K-1 helicopters in late 1957. Kaman Aircraft, based in Bloomfield, Connecticut, was founded in 1945 by Charles Kaman, and during the first ten years the company operated exclusively as a designer and manufacturer of several helicopters that set world records and achieved many aviation firsts. The K-20 design featured a four-bladed main rotor and three-bladed tail rotor with a single

General Electric T58-8F turboshaft engine. Redesignated the UH-2 in 1962, the type was initially employed from carriers in the SAR role, although the utility of the airframe saw its continual development, and the fitment of weapons was one such upgrade. From 1968, further improvements saw the remaining machines in service fitted with two T58 engines.

A milestone in the Seasprite's career was the LAMPS programme initiated in 1970, which recognised the requirement for a Light Airborne Multi-Purpose System helicopter to operate from smaller ships, independent of the carrier arm, in a tactical Anti-Submarine capacity. Known as LAMPS Mark I, the advanced sensors, processors, and display capabilities aboard the helicopter enabled ships to extend their situational awareness beyond the line-of-sight limitations that hamper shipboard radars and the short distances for acoustic detection and prosecution of underwater threats associated with hull-mounted sonars. Machines reconfigured for the LAMPS mission were redesignated SH-2D, with the first such operational aircraft joining the USS Belknap (CG-26) in December 1971. By 1973 an improved LAMPS system had been fitted to the SH-2F, which also featured upgraded engines, longer life rotor, and higher take-off weight. The Navy ordered sixty production machines in 1980, and commencing in 1987 sixteen of these were fitted with chin mounted FLIR Sensors, Chaff (AIRBOC)/Flares, dual rear mounted IR scramblers, and Missile/Mine detecting equipment.

The entire H-2 fleet was eventually upgraded to SH-2F standard, barring two airframes, with the last six on the production line finished instead as SH-2Gs - the Super Seasprite variant, which is still

A SH-2F Seasprite (BuNo 151324) from Light Helicopter Anti-submarine Squadron 35 (HSL-35) Magicians, assigned to Anti-submarine Warfare Wing Pacific, preparing to land on the helicopter pad aboard the frigate USS Cook in September 1981

ion service with some navies today.

SH-2Fs saw service in *Desert Storm* as well as other operational deployments, where the improved avionics enabled it to perform well against the surface threat as well as submarines. The aircraft retired from US Navy service in 1993, along with the last of the venerable Knox Class Frigates whose decks could not accommodate the incoming SH-60 Sea Hawk.

One enthusiastic exponent of the Seasprite has been New Zealand, which acquired six SH-2Fs from the US Navy to replace its Westland Wasp fleet. These operated from ANZAC class frigates, crewed by a mix of air force and RNZN personnel known as No. 3 Squadron RNZAF Naval Support Flight. These initial machines were replaced by five SH-2G Super Seasprites, and subsequently relegated to a training role.

Enter the Super G

The logical progression from the SH-2F was the SH-2G Super Seasprite, an improved and versatile variant whose missions include anti-submarine and anti-surface warfare, anti-ship missile defence, and anti-ship surveillance and targeting. Secondary missions may include medical evacuation, search and rescue, personnel and cargo transfer, as well as small boat interdiction, amphibious assault air support, gun fire spotting, mine detection and battle damage assessment.

The development programme commenced in 1985 when the US Navy needed an enhanced anti-submarine capability and felt upgrading current helicopters would be a more cost effective approach. The prototype was a modified SH-2F fitted with two more powerful General Electric T700-GE-401/401C engines. The newcomer boasted a reinforced upper fuselage to support the new heavier engines, as well as multifunctional displays and new avionic systems. The Super Seasprite was retired by the US Navy Reserve in 2001 but continued in service with other users.

The Royal Australian Navy began operating SH-2G(A) Super Seasprites in 2003, although the machine was not a success in RAN service. Poor foul-weather and low-light capability, among other problems, saw the type restricted initially to passenger and supply duties, and their complete grounding in 2006. Following considerable debate and prevarication, the Australian government eventually returned the machines to Kaman in 2008.

Both Egypt and the RNZN seem to have fared better, with ten aircraft bought by the Egyptians from 1997, equipped with dipping sonar, and the six New Zealand examples, fitted with different avionics to their troubled RAN neighbours, providing useful service on the ANZAC class frigates, two Offshore Patrol Vessels and *HMNZS Canterbury* Multi-Role vessel.

The Polish Navy also received four aircraft, which were included in the purchase of two Perry class frigates from the United States Navy.

51

A Royal Navy Lynx and a Royal New Zealand Navy Seasprite helicopters in formation during Exercise Bersama Lima in the South China Sea with ships from Singapore, Malaysia, New Zealand, Australia and the United Kingdom

Chapter VI

Trumpeter Kit 01626
"Wellington" MK.IC

Wellington

Gryphon Wimpey

Improving Trumpeter's 1/72 Wellington Mk Ic

By Wojciech Butrycz

To write at length on the history, service or development of this famous WWII bomber would be a waste of both space and readers' time. So much has been written here and elsewhere at length and in greater depth than we have scope for in this article, and a selection of relevant references is listed below. Several Polish squadrons flew the Wimpey with Bomber Command, and I can only regret that so far none of the well-known Polish publishers have released a decent monograph on the bomber. This has been done, at least, by the Czechs, and the 4+ Publication on the type is an essential for all modellers wishing to build a replica of the type.

In recent years, the modelling market has been flooded with Vickers Wellington kits in the most popular scales. Firstly, there were the MPM models, which were huge improvements over the aged Airfix and Matchbox releases from the past century. There were also ex-Frog moulds under Russian labels, but these were of rather both poor quality and limited availability. Altogether MPM released five versions, among them the Mk Ic, Mk X, Mk III, Mk II (with in-line

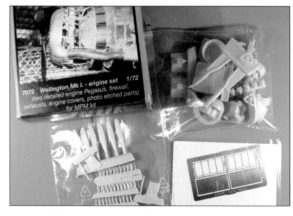

CMK set #7072 for Pegasus engines and covers

engines), and Mk VIII. For these models, several CMK update sets, combining high quality resin and etched details were then released, covering the cockpit, Pegasus engines, undercarriage elements and wells, flaps, and bomb bays.

When the first of the Trumpeter Wellington series arrived on the market in the shape of the Mk Ic it was a state-of-the-art twenty-first century model. The quality of moulding and the mass of tiny details

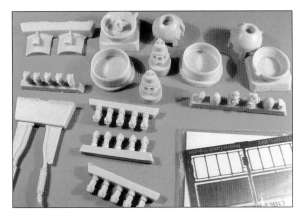
CMK's engine set really does go to town on this area of the kit

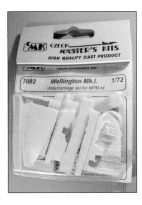
CMK's resin undercarriage set is designed for the MPM kit but can be adapted for Trumpeter's as well

Quickboost's set of Wellington gun barrels is a considerable improvement even over some very good kit items

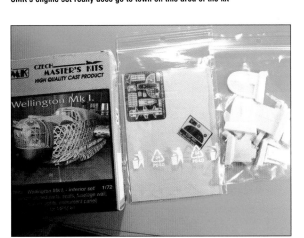
CMK set #7073 for the fuselage interior offers cockpit and other fuselage parts

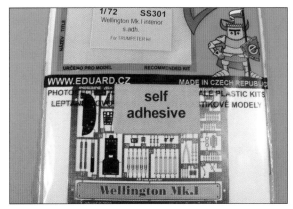
Eduard's coloured cockpit set #SS 301, consisting mainly of instrument panels and harnesses

53

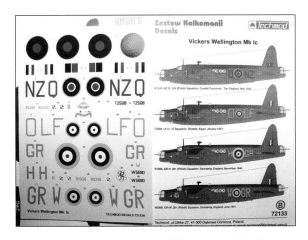
Techmod's decals, one of two released for MPM or Trumpeter Mk Ic kits

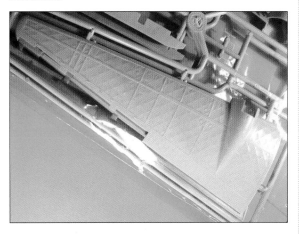
The quality of the mouldings is apparent – as is the oversized geodetic effect

did not, however, guarantee a completely accurate replica of the famous bomber, and the too-thin wheels and subsequent inaccurate undercarriage struts and wheel wells, plus the exaggerated geodetic structure, are the most prominent errors, of which more anon. These kits were followed shortly by Eduard's etched sets, including a coloured cockpit interior set, landing flaps, and bomb bay, while Quickboost has released a set of remarkable resin gun barrels. The arrival of Techmod's decal sheet for four different Wellington Mk Ics, including three of 301 and 304 (Polish) Squadrons, allowed me to get my Gryphon Wimpy project under way.

As already mentioned, the Trumpeter model is of the highest quality, typical for the Far Eastern companies, with a large amount of finely moulded details for the cockpit, crew, and bomb compartments, gun turrets, and undercarriage. This attention to detail has, however, led to an over-statement of the geodetic structure, especially on the flying surfaces. I remedied this with a

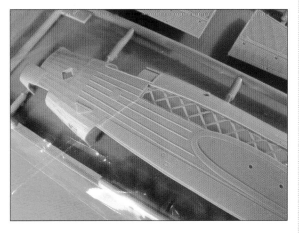
The over-emphasised geodetic structure is repeated on the fuselage, but here it is not so obvious once the model is painted in black

Remedy for the too-prominent structural detail - dense, but still self-levelling paint and... a lot of patience

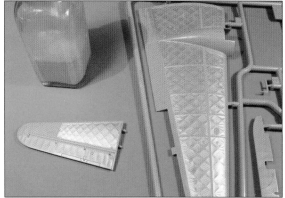

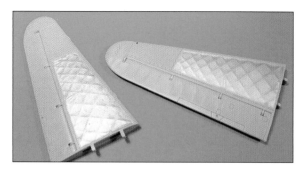

The reduced geodetic structure effect shown on the tailplane surfaces

Eduard's cockpit fret features highly realistic panels, gauges, belts etc.

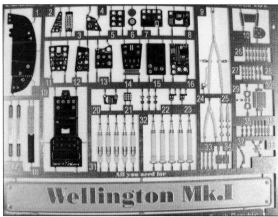

Wellington Mk.I

The completed cockpit elements including floor, seat, steering column from the kit, and instrument panels and harnesses from the Eduard set

two-stage procedure; firstly, filling all the recessed square areas with a paint mix left over from another project. The paint was quite thick but still self-levelling. It is however, a time consuming process as one can only fill areas horizontally in line, which then need to be put aside to dry before the next areas can be filled. The upper surface of the wings, consequently, needed five or six filling-and-drying sessions.

Once all the areas are filled with thick paint and have dried, the second stage simply involves sanding the areas to reduce all the raised structural details.

Once this time-consuming and boring job was done, I was able to start on the cockpit interior. For this I used a mixture of kit parts,

CMK, and Eduard sets, the latter almost in its entirety, as it includes the excellent colour instrument panels and harnesses for the crew seats. The pilot's seat floor and steering wheel and column were taken from the kit and painted black, as were the remaining two seats. Columns were painted interior grey-green. I next assembled Eduard's pre-coloured instrument panels, added throttles, levers etc. and finally all seats were given their harnesses. The floor was also treated with rust-coloured dry pastel powder, and the pilot's seat back and armrests were dry brushed with a light leather shade to give an impression of well-worn black leather.

Gun turrets made from kit parts, CMK PE elements, soft wire

Gun barrels changed, and the turret on the right is seen completed just before enclosing in its glazing

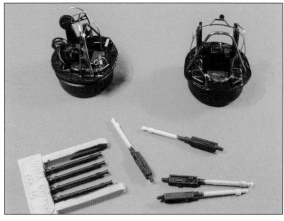

Quickboost barrels painted and ready to attach after the kit barrels are removed

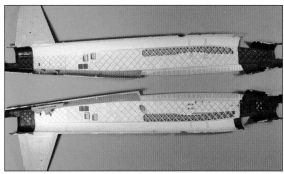

Fuselage interior painted

55

I then turned to the gun turrets, again using a mix of kit, Quickboost, and CMK details, as well as some pieces of soft wire. The finished result just goes to show how much more detail can be achieved with resin castings, over the even highest quality plastic moulding – which is why we have seen such an incredible rise in the popularity of aftermarket detail sets in recent years.

Next up were the fuselage compartments. First, the interior of the fuselage halves were painted black in the turret and cockpit areas, and buff in other departments with aluminium geodetic structure and bulkheads, and an Interior Grey-Green rear floor area. I am not sure, if all of this is correct, as there is some disagreement between existing resources and museum images. There are also some wooden tables and partition walls that needed a wood effect painted on. The kit provides a fully equipped and detailed fuselage interior, and while the addition of the Eduard instrument panels and harness is eminently desirable, especially if one is building the model with open cockpit hatches, the kit parts provided are more than sufficient for the other enclosed areas as nothing will be visible after closing the fuselage halves. I did, however, add Eduard parts and some CMK resin radio components to the interior, as well as some scratchbuilt wiring and ducting, mainly based on the excellent fuselage interior drawing in the 4+ Publication book.

With all the interior sub-assemblies completed I was able to join the fuselage halves.

Glazing was added at this point, and the cockpit transparency was glued in place with the upper hatches cut-out, as I had decided to leave these in the open position to allow for a better view of all Eduard's wonders. One thing of note is that the complicated shape of the cockpit canopy has been replicated correctly for the first time in 1/72. It matches the +4 Publication drawings perfectly.

It was now time to tackle the main undercarriage sets, which brings us to the kit's biggest problem - the wheels are too thin, which results in the gear legs also being incorrect – compared to drawings. I used CMK wheels and MPM's Wellington struts, the only alternative being surgery to the kit parts.

Wings were the next step. Careful study of the instructions is

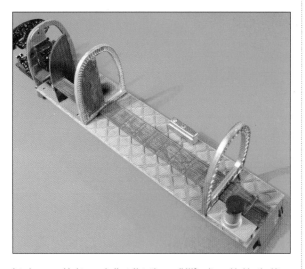

Interior assembled to good effect. Note the small WC unit provided by the kit

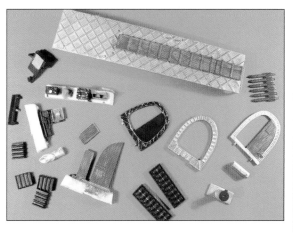

Various kit and CMK interior set items painted and awaiting addition to the interior

Close-up of the cockpit and navigator's compartment

Interior sub-assemblies shortly before gluing together

Wheels and undercarriage, highlighting the problem; light grey parts are from the kit, the others are resin CMK items, all laid over the excellent 4+ Publications 1/72 scale drawing. The errors are evident here

Pilot's cockpit glazing with cut-out area for open hatches

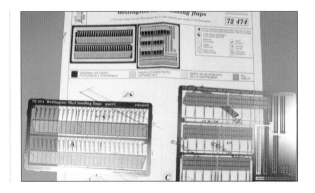

Eduard flaps set

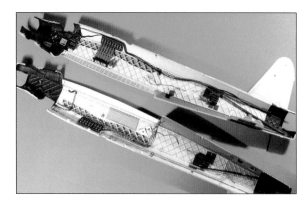

Fuselage halves inner details comprising kit, CMK, Eduard, and scratch built elements

The floor sub-assembly glued to the starboard fuselage half

advised to get the complex ailerons correctly installed before the wing halves are glued together, and the undercarriage wells also have to be installed first. I painted these black and weathered them with dry pastels, adding some hydraulic ducting from solder wire. I cut off the kit flaps, glued the wing halves together, and set them aside for drying.

Assembling the Eduard flaps is a time consuming task but worth the effort. The set consists of two large frets, and work followed the instruction sequence strictly. All the elements are fragile, and it is easy to spoil the effect, but once finished the flaps are really convincing.

Even more time-consuming was the work on the bomb bay. Eduard's set is simply gorgeous, but consists of hundreds of diminutive details, all of them easy to mislay, and eager to get lost in the carpet. For those impatient (are there such people among modellers?) I suggest CMK's resin set…or just build it with the doors closed!

Studying many pictures I noticed the bomb bay doors did not open in an even line and I assembled them correspondingly, adding more life to the finished model.

Everything was now ready for the paint session, starting with an

Fuselage put together with tailplane, antennas, and glazing in place

Undercarriage set corrected and ready to install in the wing

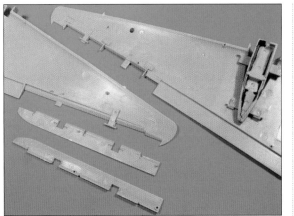

The aileron assembly is quite complicated

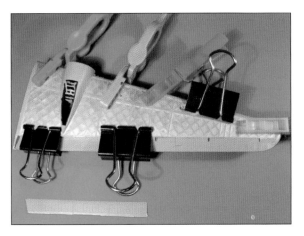

Wing put aside for drying. Note the cut-off flap area, prepared for Eduard's etched set

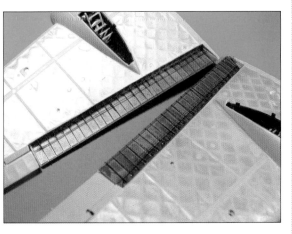

Time-consuming flap installation commences

57

Further work on the etched flaps set

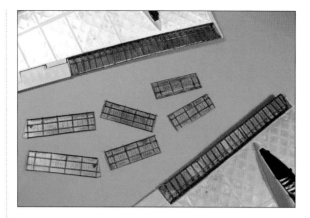

This is a major undertaking, but will be worth it in the end

The Eduard flaps complete – sit back and take a break

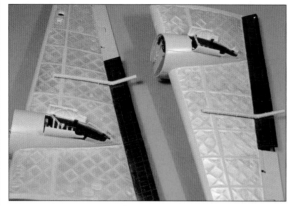

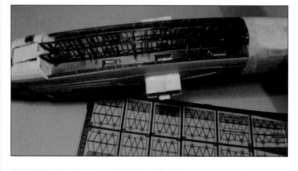

Bomb bay partly installed – just keep on following the instructions!

Eduard bomb bay set. If you thought the flaps were detailed...

application of Dark Earth to the upper surfaces. Next, I photocopied the instruction sheet, enlarged it to 1/72, and made three copies, just in case. I cut out the Dark Earth areas as masks, attaching them to the model with masking tape and sprayed overall Dark Green. Once dry, I used the same method to mask the wavy demarcation line between the upper and lower surface colours along the fuselage and sprayed all side and undersurfaces with matt black.

With all painting done, I was able to put together the fuselage and wing sub-assemblies, and start to apply decals to the model, opting for W 5690 GR°W from 301st Ziemi Pomorskiej (Polish) Squadron, Hemswell 1942, mainly due to the gryphon motif on the port side of the nose - hence the title of this article, which has nothing to do with engines!

Upper camouflage painting used an enlargement of the decal sheets instructions cut up as masks

I have only one query regarding the superb decals provided by Techmod – I am not sure if the small Polish national chessboard was really painted on the other side of the nose. Existing photographs of other Wellingtons from this squadron do not show anything painted there.

Fully decalled, the model was sprayed with Vallejo matt clear and left aside for drying, and later heavily weathered with grey, rust, and black dry pastels, referring to numerous contemporary photographs of the real aircraft, and some paint chipping, mainly in the engine nacelles area, was done with the use of a silver ball pen.

The final work on the model was to install two CMK Pegasus engines, with covers removed. I used all the CMK parts plus some solder and copper wire, small plastic parts etc. I also decided to use only one prop spinner with the other left off to show details of the CMK propeller boss. Additionally, I scratchbuilt a crew entrance ladder, which was installed to the opening below the cockpit.

Masking the fuselage using Montex masks designed for the MPM kit, supplemented by Humbrol maskol and Tamiya Masking tape

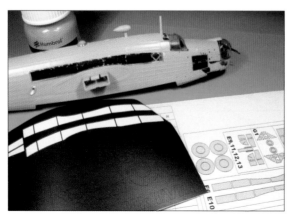

I really enjoyed building the Wimpy despite the extra work engendered by the oversized geodetic structure and thin wheels. Building up the interior was fun, but not really worth the effort of

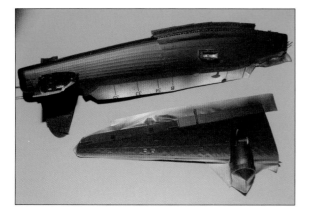

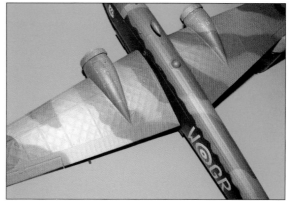

Undersuface black sprayed on after careful masking of the upper surfaces

Decalling underway

superdetailing, given the lack of visibility once the fuselage is closed.

There is no doubt this kit can be turned into a masterpiece. With rumours of a new-tool Halifax on the horizon at last, perhaps we can look forward to something equally as good.

REFERENCES
* Vickers Armstrong Wellington Medium Bomber Variants Mks I, IA, IC, II, III, IV, B Mk X, T Mk X, T Mk 10, T Mk XIX, T Mk 19 - 4+ Publication
* Wellington in Action, No 76 - Squadron/Signal Publications
* Warpaint Series No 10, Vickers Wellington - Hall park Books
* Polskie Sily Powietrzne W Wojnie 1939 – 1945 (Polish Air Force At 1939 – 1945 War) - AJ Press

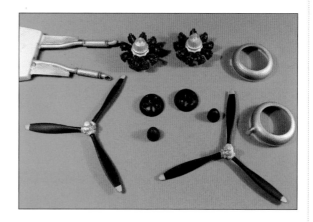

CMK engine parts assembled and painted for that final job on the open engines

59

Chapter VII

B-57B CANBERRA

Scale: 1/48	
Kit: 10104	
Type: Injection Moulded Plastic	
Manufacturer: Airfix	

Airfix Kit 10104

American Canberra

Building the Airfix B-57 Test Shot

By David Francis

Selling the Canberra to the Americans was a major coup for the British company English Electric, but there was little choice as the type easily trounced all comers in the fly-off competition held by the Pentagon. As a consolation prize Martin were given the production contract for the US Canberras and though the first example looked nearly identical to the RAF B 2 the USAF ordered a major redesign. The most obvious difference was the large tandem canopy, but there were many others, some of which Airfix have covered but some they have not.

This was the third of the Airfix Canberra test shots that we received prior to their eventual UK release. Unlike the others this kit was much nearer a production example, being moulded in Airfix's standard light grey plastic rather than the multi-coloured parts seen earlier shots. Many of the pieces look very familiar as they are identical to those in the already released B(I) 8 and this includes the

The cockpit could do with a lot of added detail or replacement

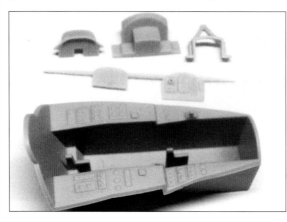

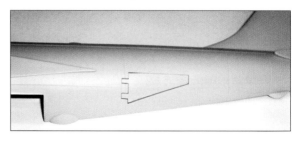

The fuselage air brakes can be posed open or closed

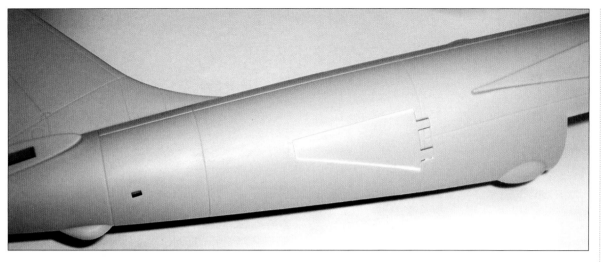

Some PVA was added around the air brake, as the gap was quite large

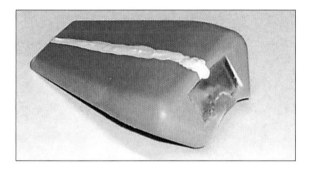

Quite a few repairs were made to the under nose bulge

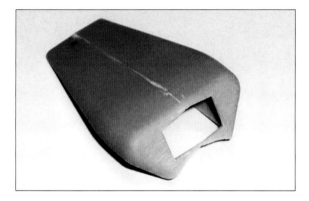

Successfully repaired and with clear part removed due to foul-up with glue

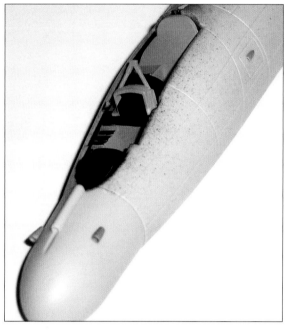

The prominent intakes need to be added

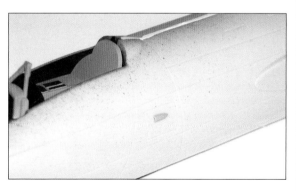

Another omission is the intake on the fuselage side

61

wings, undercarriage and weapons. Changes for the American version are confined to just two spruces. The first supplies the fuselage halves, including the cut-outs for the large air brakes on the fuselage sides and the tandem canopy of the Martin built aircraft, while the second provides most of the detail parts, including three separate nose sections for a B-57E, the RB-57E Patricia Lynn, and the night interdictor B-57G.

Just like the PR 9 and B (I) 8 the fit of all the major components is to a very high standard with only a few places requiring filler, and do bear in mind that this is not a production kit, which may fit even better. Of special note is the detail in the wheel bays, which will benefit from a little extra wiring and some carefully applied washes. Unlike British aircraft these areas and the insides of the undercarriage doors are painted in yellow zinc chromate, which adds a splash of colour. On the downside the panel lines on the fuselage appear to be a lot deeper than those on the wings and some modellers may want to fill these and rescribe them, though I think they look OK under a couple of coats of paint.

The Build

I must admit the cockpit was a bit disappointing, as the detail was very soft and at the same time very large. This is quite strange as though the previous kits were lacking in places, for the most part the detail was quite good. One thing Airfix did get right was to include two different types of ejection seat, and although basic they do look the part. The Martin designed seat was the standard model, but in the G variant and B-57s still in service during the 1970s an Escapac seat was retrofitted. I added some pre-painted Eduard seat belts to the Airfix seats which

Airfix supply a choice of parts for the front of the nacelles

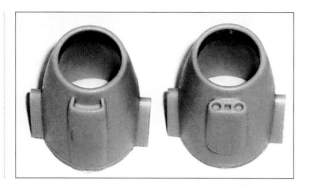

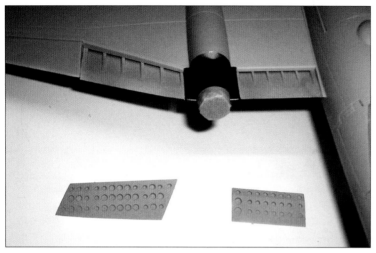

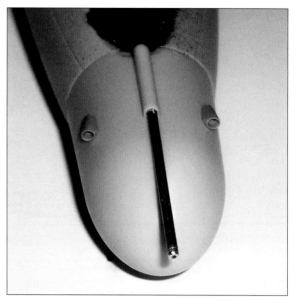

A stronger replacement probe made from brass tube

The flaps are detailed if you want to leave them open

The canopy needed to be secured in place until the glue had set

The filled rudder with its added plastic card trim tab

certainly improves their look but in time I am sure the after-market will produce a set for this kit which will be a compulsory addition to the basic kit for most modellers.

With the cockpit out of the way I now completed assembly of the wings fuselage, tail and rudder. The rudder is a standard part throughout the Airfix Canberra family, and in all versions you will have to fill the deeply engraved panel lines moulded on. You can also take this opportunity to add the missing details. In the 1960s a rectangular trim tab was added to the

Adding the aerial wire from Lycra thread

rudder of the B-57, and I reproduced this by adding a piece of very
thin plastic card between the two rudder parts. Once the glue had set
I was able to trim the plastic card to the correct shape to represent
the trim tab.

I had already decided to build the B-57G with its large bulge under
the nose, but if I had been building the standard B-57E bomber I
would also have had to make some alterations to the wings. One
change made to the Canberra by the Americans was to add guns to the
wings just outboard of the engine. Early models had four .50 cal guns
in each wing and later models replaced these with four 20mm cannon.
Airfix do not supply any parts for these or the associated ammunition
doors so it's out with the drills and a scribing tool.

The main differences between the three variants in the box are the
nose profiles, and these are supplied as separate parts to be added to
the completed fuselage and fit very well. They also are a superb place to
put the considerable amount of weight needed to prevent the B-57
from tail sitting. Before I attached the large radome of the G variant to
my fuselage I had to scribe a line around it to represent the joint. This
makes painting this section easier and I was very surprised that Airfix
had not done this for you. The large under-nose section containing the
laser markers and IR cameras on the original was slightly damaged on
my sample and I had to carry out a quick repair with Milliput before
attaching the clear part with superglue.

At this point I made my traditional mid-build muck-up. I thought I
had picked up odourless superglue, which I use to glue clear parts, but in
fact I had picked up the regular kind, which instantly released a vapour
that left a white film across the inside of the clear parts. An easy solution
to this was to add a red square of Plasticard with an Eduard RBF flag at

Eduard's pre-finished RBF tags add a little colour and disguise the glue-frosting!

the end of construction; most photos of the real plane show this item in
place to protect the glass until just before departure on a mission.

Now, Airfix have tried to produce a B-57 that covers all the major
variants in one box but without pricing it out of the market, and to do
this there have been a number of small omissions. Some, like the wing
guns, are quite easy to sort out but on my B-57G I had a real problem.

One of the most noticeable features of the G is its oversized nose
probe and the two large prominent intakes on each side. Airfix have
supplied a plastic probe but it is poorly shaped and due to its
prominent position prone to damage. A simple answer is to replace it
with one made from thin brass tube and rod which is available from
your local model railway store. The two large intakes, however, are
nowhere to be seen. I am sure that Quickboost will already be tooling a
set up as we speak, but I could not ignore this omission on my model
so had to find an alternative. Surprisingly the answer is a set
Quickboost produced last year for the Trumpeter MiG-19 (QB48156).
This supplies two large intakes that look similar to the ones fitted to the
G with a little reshaping. At the same time this set also provides a
number of intakes that are almost identical to those missing from the
port fuselage side and on the inside of each engine, which Airfix have
also missed off.

With all the major construction done I could now attach the
canopies and mask them off with Tamiya tape and use a sharp scalpel
blade to cut around the moulded frame lines before starting to paint
the final camouflage scheme.

Painting and Decals
No decals or paint guides are supplied with these test shots but I can
say that the G model was only painted in SEA camouflage over Night
Black undersides and the RB-57 Patricia Lynns were black overall, but

63

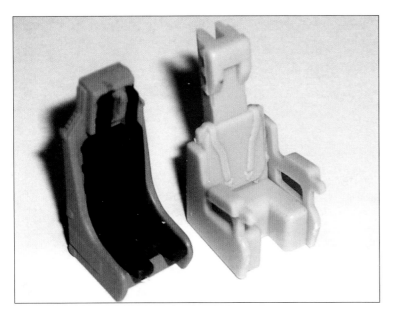

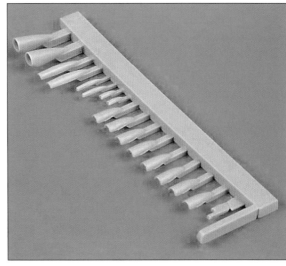

The Quickboost Mig-19 set that supplied the intakes for this build

A choice of basic ejection seats

what schemes Airfix will pick for the standard is anyone's guess – though I am sure there will be plenty of choice from decal manufacturers in due course.

You would think that painting the SEA scheme would be an easy option, especially as the official painting guide for the B-57 was available online. That was until I compared the diagram to pictures of real B-57Gs, at which point it quickly became obvious that the patterns were not the same - in fact no two aircraft matched exactly. Obviously, during their extensive refurbishment, these airframes were repainted by a modeller. Well who else would completely ignore the painting instructions?

So what you see is my interpretation of the B-57G camouflage painted using Humbrol paints thinned 60/40 with thinners and applied with a Iwata Eclipse air brush.

For decals I was fortunate in that we had just received the reissued US Letter and numbers sets reviewed in this issue, which supplied the markings for the tail while my spares box supplied the stars and bars and a selection of stencils. To finish the painting stage I added some Pro Modeller dark wash to the panel lines before applying a coat of Xtracolour matt varnish.

Final Bits

Airfix supply a couple of thick aerials for the fuselage spine, but these are probably better replaced with Plasticard, and at the same time there are a few aerials missing from both upper and lower fuselage that need to be replicated. Other prominent missing items are the large red anti-collision beacons on the upper and lower fuselage. Mine came from a set produced by CMK that includes a number of different shapes and styles moulded in red plastic. Finally to finish my model I added the wire that runs from the rudder to a post on the starboard fuselage, using my preferred Lycra thread, which is fairly robust and seems to survive most of my attempts to break it when transporting my models to shows.

Conclusion

I have highlighted a number of omissions from the Airfix B-57, and I certainly found this model a bit of a disappointment when compared to the same company's PR 9, which was far more complete out of the box. On the plus side Airfix have offered a good selection of variants with all the major work done for you, and personally I would find it easier to add small details than to produce a new nose from scratch.

At the end of the day the finished model looks like a B-57 and if you want to add on more detail there are plenty of resin and brass updates.

Upper surface plan view showing
positions of the wing walkway, USAF
lettering and national insignia

65

MARTIN RB-57E
Scale: 1/72
Kit No: 05018
Type: Injection Moulded Plastic
Manufacturer: Airfix

'Patricia Lynn'

The Airfix 1/72 scale Martin RB-57E kit – straight from the box... well almost!

By Ross Marven

I started this project a couple of weeks before the 2008 Yeovilton Show with the idea that it would be a quick 'straight-from-the-box' build for the show, as it was a single colour and I did not have the references to add too much detail anyway.

However the research soon began to take over, as it does, and a couple of hard to ignore items meant that in the end, I departed from the 'straight-from-the-box' idea and the model did not make it to the show...

Historical notes

The 'Patricia Lynn' project was supposedly named after the wife of the chief engineer who led it when he was given the option to choose the name. It began in 1963 with two B-57E aircraft, (55-4243 and 55-4245), which were modified with a KA-1 36 inch oblique camera and a Fairchild KA-56 rotary prism panoramic

camera in the nose and further cameras and an infra-red scanner in the bomb bay.

These two aircraft began operations as Detachment 1 of the 460th TRW from Tan Son Nhut in May 1963, with two more arriving in December 1964, (55-4237 and 55-4249). The RB-57E designation had previously been used for a different variant but appears to have become generally accepted for these aircraft as well. One aircraft was lost in combat on 5 August 1965 (55-4243) and a replacement (55-4264) arrived in November 1965. Typical operations were night time reconnaissance missions to identify Viet Cong camps and supply routes and bomb damage assessments.

Equipment changes were frequent with one significant upgrade in 1968, (Compass Eagle), providing a real time display for the rear crew member to monitor the infra-red scanner. This gave the RB-57E an edge over all other reconnaissance aircraft in the Vietnam Theatre as they had to return to base with their IR film and have it

A 'Patricia Lynn' RB-57E taxis in at Tan Son Nhut AB Vietnam, with a C-123 on final appraoch for landing in the background. (USAF)

One of the original delivery 'Patricia Lynn' RB-57Es in the initial natural metal finish scheme

Unidentified pilot of Detatchment 1 of the 460th Tactical Reconnaissance Wing, standing infront of his overall black finished 'Patricia Lynn' RB-57E

developed before any useful information could be obtained from it.

The RB-57E was also claimed to provide much better IR information than the RF-4C as images from the latter suffered from vibration and it could only cover a small area. Quotes in some of my references claim the RB-57Es produced about 80% of the useful photography done in Vietnam and about 94% of battlefield intelligence.

One more aircraft, (55-4264 – the replacement aircraft delivered in November 1965 and the subject of the Airfix 1/72 kit), was lost in combat on 25 October 1968 and another replacement machine, (55-4257), began combat operations in October 1968.

From 1968 through to 1970 missions included monitoring traffic on the Mekong River delta with the real-time IR proving especially useful for spotting Viet Cong sampans. In mid-1971 operations ceased and the 'Patricia Lynn' project came to an end.

Camouflage and Markings

At the beginning of the deployment the aircraft were delivered in an overall natural metal finish but they quickly changed to an overall matt black scheme, (which sometimes looked a very dark grey appearance), which was disliked by the aircrews as they felt it marked them out for special attention from the enemy.

The US AIR FORCE lettering on the side seems to have disappeared somewhere between 1966 and 1968. Tail codes sometimes appeared in red and sometimes in grey and unit badges, (either a stylised numeral '1' or a bat), were sometimes in evidence. Detail stencilling also seemed to have varied considerably between photographs. One good source is the web page 'Reconnaissance in Vietnam' by John Harris who was commander of Detachment 1 of the 460th Tactical Reconnaissance Wing at Tan Son Nhut from

December 1968 until November 1969. He quotes the interior colours of the equipment bays as varying over the years from white through to various shades of 'military' green.

The Model

The 1/72 Airfix kit seems to have most of the basic features of the B-57 variant, but the mouldings betray their origins as the British Canberra variant with pronounced steps around the 'new' nose and bomb bay, as well as their age with very thick and heavy details. One detail that caught my eye was the ejection seats which are moulded in three parts and seem basically accurate. If the mouldings had achieved scale thickness they wouldn't be out of place by today's standards.

Other interior detail seems adequate to add interest if somewhat clumsy and lacking an instrument panel to fit under the coaming supplied for the back seat. The decals for the RB-57E variant in my version of the kit, (with a black painted model on the boxtop), were for the aircraft shown in the heading photo taken from the USAF museum online fact sheet.

The details which let down the 'Patricia Lynn' version are the

The finished model – 'Patricia Lynn' RB-57E, 55-4264, of Detatchment 1 of the 460th Tactical Reconnaissance Wing based at Da Nang AB, South Vietnam, circa late 1965, (and the subject of the Airfix 1/72 kit), which was lost in combat on 25 October 1968

A 'Patricia Lynn' Martin RB-57E, serial 55-4264 at Da Nang AB, South Vietnam, January 1964. This aircraft was lost on 25 October 1968 and is the aircraft featured in the 1/72 Airfix kit. (USAF)

Air and ground crew of Detatchment 1 of the 460th Tactical Reconnaissance Wing at Da Nang AB, South Vietnam, 1964

Lt Col John Prodan and Major Kenneth V Steinharter of the 460th TRW, get the customary greeting at the end of their last RB-57 mission! (USAF)

new nose which lacks the camera ports and seems a little too bulbous and the missing pitot head from its new location above the windscreen. It was displaced from its original location by the 36 inch camera. Also there are no indications of reconnaissance equipment in the bomb bay, but I think this was mounted such that it only showed when the bomb bay door was rotated to the open position. Finally the 'E' variant had a modified tailcone associated with its designed role as a target tug.

Construction

Given that by adding the KA-1 and KA-56 camera ports and pitot head the model would no longer qualify for my local IPMS Branch's annual competition 'straight-from-the-box' class, I

decided to make one more change which I felt would enhance the appearance considerably – and engraved all the panel lines. I also thought the rubbing down associated with this would remove the moulding seams associated with the changes from the kit's previous life as a British Canberra as well as the 'Tyneside' rivets apparent in some places.

The scribing was done before the parts were assembled using the raised lines on the kit as a guide. They are heavy enough to guide a plough, let alone a scriber! In a few places I did need to use a flexible metal ruler to make sure I got straight lines around the curve of the fuselage. This must be one of the easiest kits to scribe so if you think scribing is too much like hard work this is an ideal project to convince you otherwise.

A 'Patricia Lynn'
RB-57E, 55-4245,
photographed at
Elmendorf AFB,
Alaska, in August
1967 (USAF)

Sergeant Richard L
Moser of
Detatchment 1 of
the 460th Tactical
Reconnaissance
Wing, signals the
pilot to start the
engine of a USAF
RB-57 prior to a
reconnaissance
mission (USAF)

Next came the modifications to the nose to represent the
cameras. Firstly the 36 inch KA-1 is simply represented by drilling
hole facing forwards and slightly downwards in the lower front of
the nose cone, but the KA-56 is more difficult as it is very hard to
see in photos of the RB-57E. After a lot of searching on the web I
found the same camera is also fitted to RF-4 Phantom
reconnaissance variants and that the Revell F-4F includes the
transparencies associated with the RF-4E version of the kit so I did
not need to buy a kit just for this part. In fact the Phantom part is
the whole of the lower nose for the RF-4 so the KA-36 needs to be
cut out of this part and a corresponding slot cut in the Canberra
nose cone, (see accompanying photos).

RB-57E cockpit area showing the bat style of unit badge and stencilling
(Reconnaissance in Vietnam web page)

Starboard side view of an RB-57E showing the positioning of
the ejection seat warning triangles

Despite cramming several grammes of weight in the nose area my
model was determined 'tail-sitter'. Note the tell-tale tail strut!

... fuselage underside Fairchild KA-56 rotary prism panoramic camera fairing – 'borrowed' from a Revell RF-4E kit!

Two views of the 36 inch KA-1 nose mounted and...

Modified Airfix kit nose cone

The cutout for the camera needs to extend a few millimetres into the fuselage – I'm not sure how many but I guess the rear of the camera window of the transparency should line up with the rear of the nose cone, leaving the fairing to overlap the fuselage.

Cameras on the finished model

At this point I added the nose weight – but don't believe the Airfix instructions which say two grammes, I think they mean two kilogrammes! I stuffed the nose with lead, put some under the cockpit floor and, panicking at a late stage in construction, made the bulkhead between front and rear cockpits from lead sheet – and I still had a tailsitter! Actually this is not too much of a problem as the B-57 often appears in photos with a prop under the tail, which is supplied by Airfix, but it was a bit galling after trying so hard to avoid the problem.

The remainder of the construction was 'by the book', using Light Gull Grey for the cockpit interior and Zinc Chromate Yellow for the undercarriage bays, (see the USAF museum online fact sheet photo). The last modification was done after construction – cutting the tip off the tailcone and adding a short piece of round sprue. I think the tailcone shape should really be bulked up to be a 'rounded triangle' but it's 1/72 scale and I wanted to finish the model.

Painting was with Xtracrylix Night Black. The kit decals were a bit of a pain with a tendency to silver at every opportunity and if the carrier film was trimmed they then curled up! There was,

however, no other option but to use them and they eventually settled down after several liberal applications of Micro Sol/Set and some colourful 'engineering' language. A top coat of Xtracrylix Matt Varnish gave the required matt finish.

Painting the intakes was also a challenge as they are moulded in one piece and getting the engine front silver, and the intake trunking, guide vanes and centre body white, whilst keeping a neat line between the white and the black airframe colour was beyond me.

Although it missed the February 2008 Yeovilton show, the model made it to the Plymouth show in April – something of a record for me in terms of time from start to completion!

References

Mentioning the web page makes it an ideal moment to list the references for the RB-57E. There are relatively few sources although you will find them being quoted or repeated in many places. These are the ones I found most useful...

- *Martin B-57 Canberra – the Complete Record*, by Robert Mikesh, published by Schiffer. This is an expanded version of Ian Allan's *B-57 Canberra at War* by the same author. I ordered my copy from Amazon in the US at half the price of Amazon UK after taking postage into account.
- *B-57 Canberra in Action*, Squadron/Signal series No 1077, which has a page on the RB-57E and the 'Patricia Lynn' project.
- The USAF Museum website fact sheet:
  http://www.nationalmuseum.af.mil/factsheets/factsheet.asp?fsID=2721
- The 'Reconnaissance in Vietnam' page of the B-57 Canberra website
  http://www.b-57canberra.org/reconnaissance_in_vietnam.htm

69

Chapter VIII

SOPWITH PUP

Scale: 1/72
Kit No: 01062
Type: Injection Moulded Plastic
Manufacturer: Airfix

Airfix Kit 01062

A Pair of Pups

Two colourful trainers from the venerable Airfix tool

By Dave Hooper

I have often heard the story that Sopwith's type 9901 got its name 'Pup' because of its size and resemblance in relationship to the Strutter. In fact Sopwith's first true single-seat fighter was derived from a small single-seat personal transport and aerobatic aircraft built for Sopwith's chief test pilot Harry Hawker in 1915. The Pup as it eventually came to be known was approved by the Sopwith experimental department on February 9, 1916, however it wasn't until Christmas 1916 that the first complete Pup unit, no. 54 Squadron,

reached France. This nippy little fighter immediately became a favourite with its pilots, both in the RNAS and the RFC, who revelled in its excellent handling abilities at altitude. Surprisingly in an era when a fighter aircraft's usefulness on the front line often lasted only a matter of months, the Sopwith Pup was retained in France until the end of 1917. Even then the Pup continued to be built in large quantities, mainly for use in trainer units, and the type was still in production at the time of the Armistice. A total of around 1,896 Pups were built by the time the type was declared obsolete by the RAF in December 1918.

The Kit

The Sopwith Pup is another of those classic WWI fighter aircraft designs that is long overdue an update in 1/72. The only offering we have in this scale is the venerable Airfix tooling, which first appeared on the shelves of Woolworths in 1974. I'm not sure of the current availability of this kit but it was re-released a few years ago and is generally easy to find. The kit itself was the last WWI aviation subject that Airfix released and is generally regarded as their best, but even so there are a number of modifications that can be made to improve the

Scratchbuilt internal detail. The Wicker seat is made from fabric hardened with superglue

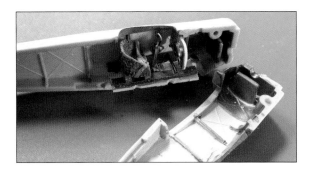
The interior detail is painted and fitted

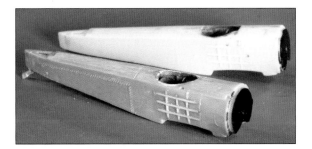
The fuselage halves are closed

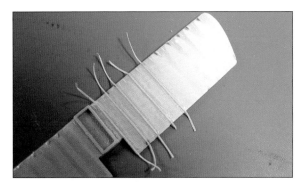
Rib tape detail is added to the rubbed-down wings using masking tape

The Blue Rider decal sheet

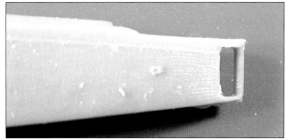
The aft tip of the fuselage is modified to include a kingpost

The Le Rhone engines are modified from Revell E.III spares

accuracy, and these are all comprehensively listed by Ray Rimmel in the back of the Sopwith Pup Datafile Special. I have two editions of the Airfix Pup in my stash; one dates I would guess from the early eighties and is moulded in a light yellow plastic. The second, in a grey plastic, was purchased about fifteen years ago. As one would expect the earlier edition shows a slightly sharper quality of moulding, however both versions are reasonably clean of flash and defects.

Decals

Each kit comes with a small decal sheet but neither is that inspiring. Luckily Blue Rider came to the rescue some years ago with a couple of sheets allowing the modeller to attempt some of the many colourful trainer pups from WWI. It was the second sheet that I intended to use for my pair. This contains two options, B7575 A chequerboard black and white coloured trainer, and C272 which had red white and blue strips across its fuselage. Visually the decals are well printed and very attractive.

The Fuselage

My first task was to carry out some basic modifications to the fuselage halves. As detailed in the Windsock special the stringer detail each side of the cockpit is incorrect. While Ray suggests removing it, I decided to go one step further and replace it. This was done by gluing very thin strips of 10 thou Plasticard onto the fuselage in a kind of noughts and crosses pattern. Once in place these were then sanded down until the protrusion from the fuselage was very slight. A

triangular exhaust channel was also opened out on the underside of the forward fuselage using a razor saw. Very little remedial work was required here as the plastic was just about thick enough to accept the removal of a channel without leaving too big a hole in the centre.

Work then began on the internal cockpit. For its day the original Airfix cockpit is actually quite good, but once again I decided to go the extra yard, throw out what I had and start from scratch. A floor was made from scrap Plasticard while the wicker bucket seat was manufactured from pieces of rough fabric, hardened with superglue. Strips of masking tape were added to depict the seatbelt. The instrument panel was again made from Plasticard while the dials were cut from various sizes of plastic tubing, and to this I added an Aeroclub control column and photo etch throttle for each of the Pups. All these parts were then painted, fitted into position and the fuselage halves closed.

As documented in the Windsock special the Pup had a king post in the tail of the fuselage. In order to create this I used Ray Rimmel's suggested method of filing out a slot in the rear fuselage and then adding a small piece of plastic rod to the tip.

Lower Wing and Tail

As with most older WWI models the flying surfaces of Airfix's Pup are very overdone and my first job was to attempt to improve the appearance of the wings. I began by sanding away all that heavy rib detail until the surface was almost flat. The effect this gave was satisfactory for the undersides of the wings and tail section, but not

Some filler will be needed around the cowling

The lower wing, tailplane and engine are fitted

The metal forward fuselage and cowling is masked off and painted

For C272 the fuselage roundel and white fuselage stripe were replaced due to the translucency of the decals

perfect for the uppersides. After scratching my head for a while on how to improve this I decided to try gluing very thin strips of Tamiya masking tape across the upper surfaces of the wings to represent rib tapes. This was done once the wing had been glued into position. It does still looks a tad heavy to me and I do wonder whether I've wasted a few nights replacing one abomination with another one, but the deed is now done and I have at least managed to reduce the level of sag of the wings. Perhaps next time I will try using decal film for the rib tapes.

If the tail is fitted in the position intended you will find that its position is a little further back than it should be. To rectify this, the slot was cut away on the tailplane, and the corresponding recess on the fuselage was extended by approximately 2mm. Before fitting the tail I scored the elevator hinge line with a scalpel, bent the elevator downwards and sealed it into position with some liquid poly.

The Engine

Both of the trainers that I was attempting to build were powered by 80hp Le Rhone engines. While the kit engines would make reasonable

representations of the Le Rhone Rotary they are a little on the small side, so I began hunting through my spares box for some suitable replacements. After a few false starts I eventually settled on using a pair of engines that originally came from the Revell Fokker E.III kit. These items were modified by flattening the centre of the engine and gluing a Plasticard disc with rivet detail pressed outwards on top. The engine was painted and glued into position and the two-part cowling cleaned up and fitted.

Painting and Decalling

Now I could begin the painting and decalling process. C272 was relatively easy as all it required was a few coats of homemade PC10. The cowling could either be black or red (In black and white Orthochromatic photographic of the time red always looks black). In

To make it easier to fit the checkerboard fuselage markings the decals were cut into three sections

Cabane struts made from brass strutz are added

Rigging is dry fitted using masking tape before committing to glue

The completed checkerboard fuselage and lower wing

The upper wings and interplane struts are fitted

The upper wing of B7575 is painted white ready for decalling

73

keeping with the colourful appearance of the aircraft I felt red to be the more likely option. The metal forward fuselage area was painted silver, washed using a Citadel black wash and dry brushed with silver.

I painted B7575 white all over in readiness for the checkerboard decals. The cowling and forward fuselage were painted silver in the same manner as C272, while the wood upper decking was built up using various browns and beiges.

The decals turned out to be more problematic than I expected. The first thing I noticed was that they were exceptionally translucent to the point where most of the C272 decals were unusable in their original state as all the white areas looked pale green on top of the PC10. I got around this problem by replacing the roundels and adding a strip of white decal paper on top of the red, white and blue fuselage stripes. The second issue with the decals was one of conformity. No matter what softening solutions I threw at them I struggled to get them to conform to the shape of the model. The third and final problem I had was adhesion, which was very poor, especially when it came to applying the checkerboard wing decals. I got round this problem by painting a layer of PVA glue on to the surface of the wing prior to decal application.

On the plus side the checkerboard decals fitted extremely well but once applied I had the same issue with translucency for the roundels as on the C272 decals. This time I placed a disk of white decal paper under the roundels to block out the black and white squares that were showing through.

As these are both trainer Pups no guns need to be fitted, however I did add a windscreen to each model. Before adding this it is worth checking any photographic references you have as it appears that a variety of different shaped windscreens were used on Pups.

The Upper Wing

The upper wing has slotted recesses to fit the struts in. This is a great system for beginners but it does make cleaning up of the underside of the top wing extremely difficult once the part has been fitted. I therefore decided to fill in the slots, drill new holes and fit replacement brass Strutz.

At this point all my rigging location points on the wings and fuselage were drilled out. With regards to fitting the top wing I followed my usual system of fitting the cabane struts first, aligning and gluing the top wing to these. Once completely dry, interplane struts were sized and slotted into position between the two wings. I then commence rigging, which isn't too demanding on the Pup, and

Disks of white decal paper are cut out to fit under the translucent Blue Rider decals

The upper wings painted and decalled

for this I use smoke coloured invisible thread, which I find ideal for use on 1/72 or 1/48 scale models. Each length of thread was fitted through the pre-drilled location holes, pulled tight and glued.

I tend to dry fit the rigging first using masking tape just to make sure that everything is correctly positioned and nothing has been missed. Once the glue has completely dried, excess thread is cut away and the outsides of each wing (lower and upper) were cleaned up.

The remaining decal roundels were added. Control horns made from flattened plastic rod were added to the Ailerons, elevator and rudder before adding all the control wires, which is perhaps my least favourite job.

The undercarriage is fitted in to position

The Undercarriage and Final Details

With regards to shape and size the kit undercarriage struts aren't too bad. I did flatten them slightly but other than this I used them straight from the box. I did create replacement axles from pieces of strut from my spares box as the original was too large. Tail skids, which I had originally cut from the fuselages, were replaced with parts made from square profiled plastic rod. The wheels were slightly modified by cutting down the axle tips, while spare photo-etch propeller bosses were fitted to the centre of each prop. Finally pitot tubes were made from fuse wire and masking tape.

Conclusion

Despite being over thirty years old the Airfix Pup is still a very serviceable kit, the biggest drawback being the heavy flying surfaces. I have to admit to being slightly disappointed with the Blue Rider decals concerning their use and functionality, especially when they were slightly more expensive than the original kits, however they are not unusable. I'm not sure how easily available they are now, although at the time of writing they are still listed in the Hannants catalogue.

In its original form the Airfix kit is nice and simple to build and would therefore be an excellent inexpensive starting point for anyone wishing to cut their teeth on the WWI genre, and I can certainly remember building a few in my youth.

Pup Parade

Some detail views of the RAF Museum's example

Photos by Dave Hooper

A ccording to the RAF Museum's database 'Sopwith Pup N5182 was built by Sopwith Aviation Co at Kingston-upon-Thames, but delivered from Brooklands. One of a batch of 20 aircraft ordered under contractors number C.P.119901/16, serials N5180 to N5199, with 80 HP Le Rhone rotary engine. One of a total of 64 Pups built in 1916.'

The aircraft was delivered in September 1916 and entered service with C Sqn, No.1 Wing RNAS (which later became No.3 [Naval] Squadron RNAS) at Dunkirk.

A626 was one of the earliest RFC Pups to be built. She served with Naval 8 until 4th January 1917 when she was captured north of Rheims

Pups on the Western Front

The diminutive Sopwith scout's career over the trenches

By Dave Hooper

3691

On May 28th 1916, the Sopwith Scout type 9901 prototype, serial number 3691, arrived at RNAS Dunkerque for evaluation. During World War One this was standard practice, with the duration between initial acceptance of a prototype and arrival at the front often being very short. Sopwith's next project, for example, the Triplane prototype N500, was passed by Sopwith's experimental department on the day that 3691 arrived in Dunkerque.

In contrast to the Triplane the Sopwith Scout 9901 spent an unusually long period in England. Records show that she was passed by the Sopwith Experimental Department three months earlier on 9th February 1916, and RNAS trials in March reported that 'This machine is remarkable for its performance, ease of handling and for the quickness with which it can be manoeuvred. It is easy to land, landing at from 25 to 30 mph'. 3691 then sent some time at the Central flying school in Uphaven, Chingford and the Isle of Grain before finally arriving in France at the end of May.

The new Sopwith scout began its service life as part of No.5 Flight, 'A' squadron based in Coudekerque a few days later. In these early days it is likely that the machine would have been passed around between pilots in order to allow as many flyers as possible to gain experience with the new type. The aircraft drew first blood on 22nd September 1916, when Australian born Flt Sub-Lt Stan Goble sent an LVG C-type two-seater out of control.

By this time the first production aircraft had arrived to join 3691 at St Pol and the following month the prototype scout was returned to Dunkerque for modifications, which are thought to have brought it up to near production standard. Shortly afterwards 3691 was transferred to the newly formed Naval 8, based at Vert Galand farm, for service alongside the RFC on the Somme.

On Boxing Day 1916 Sub-Lt N.E.Woods, flying 3691, was involved in the downing of a Halberstadt over Bapaume, a victory that was shared with N5197, a Sopwith-built Pup from the first production batch. A few weeks later operations at Vert Galand were taken over by Naval 3, who inherited Naval 8's battle-worn Pups, however 3691 didn't remain on the squadron roster for very long and was back for repairs in Dunkerque on February 10th 1917 following an accident during take-off involving future ace Flt Sub-Lt. Len 'Titch' Rochford; 'When taking off, the tips of the propeller blades struck the ground. As soon as I was airborne there was a violent vibration throughout the machine, and it felt as though it was going to fall to pieces'.

Repaired and returned to England, 3691 flew with the Home Defence at Dover and on May 26th 1917, by now the mount of Flt Sub-Lt R.F.S.Leslie, she attacked one of a group of Gothas without result. After a long and varied career 3691 was shipped over to America as part of a fund raising exhibition and on return to her homeland was earmarked for preservation, but for whatever reason this did not happen and she was eventually scrapped.

The Strutter's Pup

The Sopwith scout's unofficial nickname is famously said to have derived from a comment by Brig. General Brancker, who on seeing the new scout next to a Sopwith 1½ Strutter commented 'Good God! Your 1½ Strutter has had a Pup'. The nickname stuck, even when officials tried to censor the use of such an undignified title.

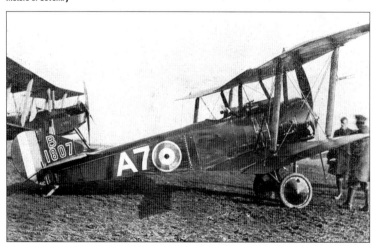

B1807, one of a large number of Pups manufactured by Standard Motors of Coventry

N6172 'Black Tulip' was captured intact on 12th April 1917

The Pup was regarded with genuine affection by those who flew it, even though the type was at a performance disadvantage compared to the Albatros Scouts it often opposed. Major James McCudden described the aircraft as a 'remarkably fine machine for general all round flying'. In his book Sopwith Scout 7309, Sir Gordon Taylor gave a more practical summary; 'Nothing much was said about the quality and performance of the Sopwith, but there was from the beginning in 66 Squadron an acceptance of the truth. Our reaction to this however, was to feel a fierce loyalty to the Pup right from the beginning. This loyalty grew into a protective instinct that would tolerate no outside criticism of the machine at all'.

A6158

Sopwith Scout A6158 was part of a contract for 100 Pups to be built at Whitehead aircraft Ltd based in Richmond. Once completed she was sent to Farnborough where she was submitted for inspection by the Aircraft Inspection Department on 19th February 1917.

Although A6158 was part of an RFC contract, and therefore initially allocated to the Expeditionary Force, she was issued to RNAS Naval 3 Squadron, based at Vert Galand, on 16th March. Just over two weeks later, on 6th April, then flown by Flt Sub-Lt Joseph Fall, she was involved in fighting over Bourlon Wood. Fall, who was destined to become one of the RNAS's top aces reported: 'Our formation was attacked by four hostile aircraft. One dived at me from in front and carried on diving. I did a half loop and dived too, following him down to 4,000 ft. I fired fifty rounds at him, saw many tracers enter his fuselage and he went down out of control. From about 1,000 ft he spun to the ground and I saw him crash'. The victim, identified as a Halberstadt D.II single seat scout, was the first of eleven enemy aircraft downed by Joseph Fall while flying Pups between April and July 1917.

Five days later Fall was again flying A6158, escorting B.E.2s over Cambrai, when the bombers were attacked by Albatros Scouts. 'I attacked a hostile aircraft head on at about 8,000 ft. I saw many tracers go into his engine as we closed on one another, I half looped to one side of him and then the hostile aircraft dived with a large trail of blue smoke. I dived after him down to about 4,000 feet and fired about fifty rounds when he went down absolutely out of control'. Fall

was then attacked by three more Albatros D.IIs and was driven down to 200ft: 'We were firing at one another whenever possible, when at last I got into a good position and attacked one from above and from the right. I closed on him, turning in behind him and got so close to him that the pilots head filled the small ring in the Aldis sight. I saw three tracers actually go into the pilots head; the hostile aircraft then simply heeled over and went to the ground. The other two machines cleared off'.

With no more enemy aircraft in sight Fall headed home remaining at low altitude. Flying so low over enemy territory he must have appeared an inviting target to German aircraft in the vicinity and he was soon harassed by a lone Halberstadt fighter: 'as he closed on me I rocked my machine until he was within fifty yards. I side-looped over him and fired a short burst at him. He seemed to clear off and then attacked me again'. This continued until Fall was in sight of the German lines: 'I looped straight over him and coming out of a loop I dived at him and fired a good long burst. I saw nearly all the tracers go into the pilot's back, just on the edge of the cockpit. He immediately dived straight into the ground'. As a result of this action A6158 was badly shot up and Fall landed at the first aerodrome he found. A week later A6158 arrived at Candas air depot, presumably for repair.

She was recorded back on strength with Naval 3 in early May but two weeks later was shot down over the German side of the line and the Pilot, FSL W.R. Walker, became a prisoner of war. Joseph Fall was awarded a DSC for his actions. He survived the Great War with a total of thirty-six victories.

RNAS Pups on the Western Front

Production Pups began arriving in France in September 1916 with 'C' Squadron of No.1 Wing being the first to receive the new type. In October the newly created Naval 8 took charge of a flight of Pups from 'C' squadron (which was by now designated No.3 Wing). The squadron was fully equipped with Pups by December and served with distinction in the Somme sector of operations. Stan Goble described the work of the Pups during this period; 'All offensive patrols were carried out at high altitudes, with the objective of engaging the enemy aircraft between the heights of 10,000 and

77

B1777 'British Guiana No.2' named 'Chin Chow' was flown by Lt. Arthur Lee in which he claimed five victories while flying with No.46 sqn. Note that the 'Chin Chow' inscription has been painted over suggesting that the photograph was taken mid-September 1917

20,000 feet. The duration of the patrols was normally three hours, which, in the opinion of all the pilots, was too long a period at which to patrol at high altitudes, with much diving and climbing, and without oxygen or electrically heated clothing. It appeared to sap our nervous energy and all pilots felt the strain'.

Nevertheless Naval 8 pilots such as Stan Goble, Bob Little, John Malone and Murray Galbraith helped the unit attain a very respectable tally. In January 1917 Naval 3, by now re-equipped with Pups, replaced Naval 8 at Vert Galand. Future aces such as Collishaw, Fall and Glen all flew with Naval 3 during this period.

In February Naval 9, based at St Pol, began to receive Pups, which were often sent up to catch German bombers on their return flight from bombing targets in England. Shortly after, Naval 4 began their brief but fruitful association with the Pup, which resulted in fourteen victories in five weeks, but by the end of July RNAS Pups had been almost completely phased out of front-line service. Len Roachford wrote 'A trip to Wimereux provided me with my last flight in a Sopwith Pup for by the middle of July the Sopwith Camel had completely replaced our Pups. Although the Pup was a delightful little aeroplane to fly, the Camel was undoubtedly a much superior fighting machine'.

A7309

A7309 was part of a second batch of fifty pups ordered from The Standard Motor Company, Coventry by the RFC in 1916. She was listed as being held at the Aircraft Acceptance Park in Coventry on 12th January 1917. It is not known when she arrived in France but she is listed as being on the strength of the newly arrived No.66 Squadron on 22nd March. Gordon Taylor recalls that he took charge of her at St Omer on his arrival in France midway through March; 'There I took over a new machine, and flew it to Vert Galand Farm. She flew well, was brand new, and had a tight, well balanced feel about her. By the time I brought her in to land I had decided to try

and keep 7309 as my personal aeroplane'.

Gordon Taylor did indeed get his wish and after 'ten days of training and acclimatization' he flew A7309 on his first Patrol over the Bapaume-Arras-Lens sector. Gordon found his early experiences of combat frustrating and victory did not come easily. He later wrote; 'I could see that fighting the Sopwith Scout against the Albatros Scout was going to be a scientific affair, needing careful thought as well as careful flying and shooting. I had been given clear evidence that my machine could turn inside the Albatros, also that the latter could outclimb me easily at 14,000 feet. I knew that its speed was noticeably greater than that of the Sopwith, so that it could also leave me standing in a dive. These factors made surprise attack absolutely essential, going in from above without being seen, using height to overcome the deficiency in level speed, and then trying to lure the heavy Albatros into a close duel'.

Gordon Taylor achieved three victories in A7309, the first occurring on 7th May when he forced an Albatros to land south of Oppy. His second victory occurred one month later, shortly after No. 66 Squadron had moved to Estree Blanche. This time an Albatros two-seater was sent out of control over Gheluvelt. A week later on the 15th June Taylor's flight again encountered Albatros C-types: 'My Hun didn't see me till I was right in position for attack; or he may not have seen me at all. After my short gunburst his nose went down and he dived vertically for the earth'.

On the 25th June, A7309 was withdrawn from active service and taken to No.1 Aircraft Depot. Taylor later wrote 'I had managed to keep 7309 well beyond the time when any aeroplane that had survived more than one hundred hours flying in France was normally returned to the aircraft depot, to be rebuilt or sent back to England as a training machine. This may seem a very short life for an aeroplane but was, in fact, considerably longer than most pilots on the Western Front'. Taylor's Sopwith Scout remained at No.2 Scout School at Candos until early 1918. It is not known when she was finally deleted although she was on record at an aircraft supply depot in April 1918.

RFC Units on the Western Front

The RFC was swift to show interest in the Pup and by the end of April had tendered a contract for a batch of fifty Pups to the Standard Motor Co. Ltd of Coventry. The first RFC Pup, A626, was completed by 27th September 1916 and sent to the Central Flying School for testing. Subsequent early production aircraft were allotted to No.54 Squadron, who by the end of December had twenty-six aircraft on strength.

No.54 Squadron was sent to France on Christmas Eve 1916 where it was eventually to be based at Chipilly. The unit's first success came on 25th January when Capt. Alan Lee in A635 drove down an

Sopwith scout prototype 3691 at RNAS Dunkerque, 1916. Note the tricolour elevators

B1727 'Normie', named by 2nd Lt Norman Dimmock, flew with No.46 Sqn from June 1917. She later had some success when Lt J.H.Cooper shared a claim for an Albatros D.V

Albatros D.II out of control north of Peronne. Twenty minutes later Lee forced a two-seater to land on the Allied side of the lines.

No.66 Squadron was the second RFC unit to be equipped with Pups on the Western Front. Formed in Filton in June 1916, the unit received its first examples in February 1917 before moving to France at the beginning of March and commencing operations a month later, taking part in the Battle of Arras. The squadron moved to Estree Blanche at the end of May for the build-up to the Battle of Messines.

No.46 Squadron began receiving Pups in April 1917. The squadron had been in France since October 1916, however a change in role resulted in the unit's Nieuport two-seaters being replaced with the scouts. Unlike the RNAS, who had phased the Pup out of front-line service by July 1917, the RFC continued to use the type on the Western front until December 1917. In the *Sopwith Pup Datafile Special* the late Jack Bruce estimates that RFC Pups outnumbered RNAS Pups by about six to one, although how many of the 1,770 Pups built before the armistice served on the front is unknown.

Air Vice Marshall Arthur Gould Lee, who flew with No.46 squadron, assessed the Pup's virtues as a combat aircraft: 'So docile a creature was meant to be flown for fun, not for killing, and in France she was never a Hungetter like the Camel I was to fly later. Yet despite her deficiencies for aggressive fighting, the Pup, at all heights, could be as evasive as a butterfly'.

References:

- *The Sopwith Pup* - J.M.Bruce, Gorgon Page, Ray Sturtivant
- *Sopwith Pup Aces of World War One* - Norman Franks
- *Sopwith Pup Datafile Special* - J.M.Bruce
- *Sopwith Scout A7309* - Sir Gordon Taylor
- *Flying Fury, Five years in the Royal Flying Corps* - James T.McCudden
- *Royal Navy Aircraft serials and units 1911 - 1919* - Ray Sturtivant, Gordon Page
- Special thanks to Roger Tisdale and Tim Upson Smith for all the kind help and encouragement given during the writing of this article.
- Cross and Cockade international produces a quarterly journal of articles on WW1 aviation. For more information - www.crossandcockade.com

N6181 'Happy 'in which Flt Cdr Lloyd Breadner of Naval 3 claimed five of his seven Pup victories

Chapter IX

'Summat for nowt'

Seafire from the spares box

By Andy Brook

Spares Box Conception

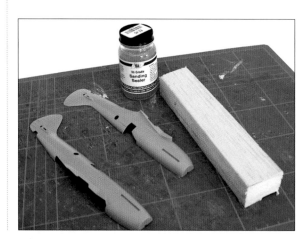

The Academy Mk XIV fuselage, the block of balsa and the sanding sealer

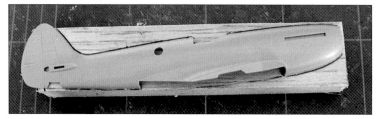

It was quicker and easier to draw around the Academy fuselage to give the shape

This particular project started when I opened the Airfix Spitfire Mk IX kit to find it came with two sets of wings. There was a challenge: what can I make with those?

I'm sure most modellers will have a spares box like mine. I've been making Spits for some years now, so have accumulated an impressive, but largely useless, collection of Vokes and Aboukir filters, cockpit windscreens and canopies, and rudders and tailplanes from various manufacturers. What I did not have was a fuselage. Cannibalising another kit, even a cheap one, would have left me with the same problem: what to do with a leftover set of wings. So, whilst the brain was working through the options, not all of them feasible (whittle a piece of wood….take a cast….plaster of Paris….plaster bandage….Polyfilla….DIY vacuum forming….crash moulding), I thought through which mark of the Spitfire family not already in my collection could I model with a C or E wing, and compared this with what was in the spares box.

Some time before, however, I'd cut out a photo of Kennett Aviation's recently restored Seafire Mk 17 SX336 on its first flight after

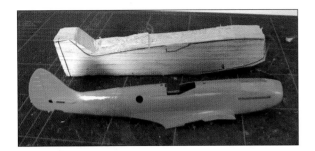

Once marked, it was out with the razor saw...

Mark out the shape, trim a bit...

Mark, trim and sand and so on...

The end result looked like a low backed Spitfire or Seafire and its dimensions matched the Mk XIV original and the plans

Some balsa was carefully cut away so the wing would sit flush with the bottom of the fuselage

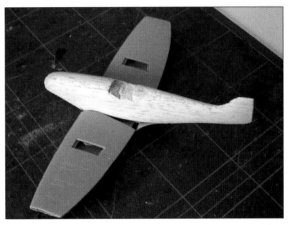

There were some pretty big gaps between the fuselage and the top of the wing, but plastic card and filler would sort those out

81

restoration. That high demarcation paint scheme on Seafires has always looked great to me, and that provided the prompt: I'd make a Griffon-engined Mk 17. In my wardrobe I had an unmade Academy Mk XIVe. I know this kit's nose profile looks a bit odd, but it would provide the right basic shape to reproduce for the Mk 17's fuselage. I just had to work out how.

After, literally, weeks of deliberation, and having ruled out everything else, the only realistic DIY option I had left was to carve the fuselage out of wood. As it happened, I had a piece of balsa in the garage, bought for some long-forgotten project, of just the right profile. So, the good news was it wasn't going to cost me any money. The bad news was that, in my experience, balsa is best described as 'hairy', however well it's rubbed down, and it soaks up paint like a sponge. Or so I thought. A visit to my local model shop, which caters for the full range of the modelling community, produced 'Hi Grade Sanding Sealer', a few coats of which, so I was assured, would help achieve the smooth finish modellers love, and a surface that would take normal modelling paints. The smallest bottle cost me £2.50, but it was still cheaper than the other options (and I would have lots of it left).

It was time now to bring together the various bits and pieces needed and to work out how to adapt or scratch-build what I didn't already have. The spares came from a variety of kits, but the new Airfix Mk I

gave me what I really needed, which was the bubble canopy. Why Airfix give you this with a Mk I (and the Mk IX too) is a mystery to me, but I'm not about to complain. Unlike the Academy bubble canopy, it doesn't have an unsightly seam down the middle, so would be perfect for the job.

The Balsa Fuselage

I had, by this time, accepted that I would probably not be able to produce a completely accurate replica, but I was aiming at something that would capture the look and the feel of a Mk 17. After all, this was going to sit on a window ledge at home, to be admired by me and the window cleaner; it was not about to grace a competition table. So, with that in mind, I started.

First step was to use a combination of the Academy Mk XIVe and the plans in the SAM *Spitfire DataFile* to mark out the right shape and dimensions on the block of balsa. Usefully, Part 1 has 1/48 plans, but this was good only for everything behind the engine. Part 2 has 1/72 plans, but they needed to be scaled up. 'Measure twice, cut once' is the watchword here, and once I'd got what seemed right, it was out with the razor saw, craft knife and various grades of sandpaper. It took an evening's quiet work to get from the rough block to the final shape I was happy with. There's probably a bit more off the port side of the

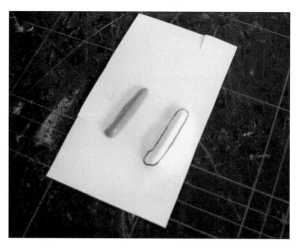

An acceptable copy of the starboard cowling bulge, ready for cutting out, with the kit part for comparison

I had used some plastic card to produce the wing fillets

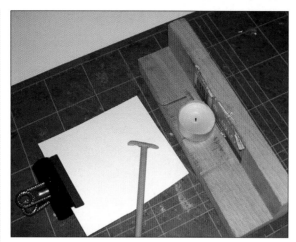

Crash moulding using a bulldog clip and a wooden mitre block for support, a small candle and some plastic card. The master is the kit part from the Academy Mk XIVe, with a pencil for a handle held on by Blu-Tack

THE NAMING OF PARTS	
Fuselage:	Balsa wood
Wings:	Airfix Mk IX
Wingtips:	ICM Mk VII or VIII
Flaps:	Plastic card
Rudder:	Plastic card sandwich
Tailplanes:	ICM
Propeller:	Airfix Mk I (4-blade)
Spinner:	Airfix Mk V (3-blade, modified)
Radiator/Oil cooler:	Aifix
Cockpit windscreen and canopy:	Airfix Mk I
Pilot:	Airfix
Pilot's seat:	Heritage Aviation Models PRXIX resin and plastic card
Tailwheel:	Airfix Mk I
Tailwheel covers:	ICM
Main wheels:	Airfix
Undercarriage:	Plastic scratch-built
Main wheel covers:	Airfix
Carburettor:	Airfix
Centre-line fuel tank:	Airfix Mk 46/47
Rockets:	Airfix Mk 46/47
Guns:	ICM
Exhaust manifolds:	Monogram P51D
Gunsight:	Airfix
Cockpit door:	ICM
Stinger hook:	Wire from scratch
Arrestor wire guard:	Wire from scratch
Pitot – port wing:	Airfix
Aerials – under starboard wing:	Airfix aerials cut down
Fuselage whip aerial:	Shaving brush bristle

nose than I would have liked and the tail is a bit lumpy, but, overall, it looks pretty good to me.

Being solid balsa, there was no hole in the middle and, thus, no cockpit. Having marked out the location, and left a fair bit of margin for slips, I used a mini-drill to ream out a suitably sized hole. That was fine, except it was very rough and ready, with over-thick sides and with no obvious way, to me, of smartening up the interior. I could have dealt with the problem by modelling the canopy shut, but I wanted to recreate the look in a number of photographs of Seafires taxiing or on a carrier's flight deck, in which the hood was open. So, I replaced the starboard side of the cockpit with a bit of plastic card, suitably smoothed in with filler, and the port side with a spare cockpit door. This had the effect of thinning down the top sills (which would be obvious with the canopy in the open position), and giving a bit of detail to distract the eye on the port side.

My solution to the problem of the roughness of the cockpit hole was to fill most of it with a pilot. The seat itself was a resin part I had not felt brave enough to cut from its mould when I made the Heritage Aviation Models PR.XIX, with some plastic card for the armour plate behind. Once on the seat, with the Airfix pilot's legs amputated below the knee to make the assembly fit properly, and with a scratch-built stick in his hands, the objective was achieved. I had thought that painting the cockpit was going to be difficult, but a bit of interior green and black in the right places, followed by some dry-brushing of aluminium on the lumpy cockpit front, produced something that looked sufficiently like an instrument panel and a result that would bear scrutiny.

It was at this point that I used the Sanding Sealer. The trick is that you rub down the balsa with fine sandpaper as smoothly as you can. Then you paint on the Sanding Sealer. Once dry, which doesn't take long, it raises the 'hairy' bits, which you sand off, and then you repeat the process until you're happy. The result is a perfectly smooth surface, which matches the plastic, with a glossy varnish finish, which will accept paint.

I decided to try scribing some panel lines for detail, only to regret it pretty quickly. The problem with balsa is that you need to use something substantial to create an effect. All I achieved was a set of over-scale trenches, which did nothing to enhance the model, and most of which I had to fill and rub down and paint on another coat of Sanding Sealer. As a result, the model is, unfortunately, largely devoid of

panel lines, some of which, especially around the nose, are quite noticeable on a Seafire.

Wings and Things

After I had retrieved that situation, it was time to turn my attention to the wings. I filled the holes in the underside of the Mk IX wing to make it right for a Mk 17, scribed on some lines to represent the wing fold, and made new flaps from plastic card. All was going well, until it came to fitting the ICM wing tips to the Airfix wing. The width was fine, but unfortunately the ICM parts were considerably thinner than the Airfix and I had a large step to deal with. This took quite a bit of rubbing down, filling and rubbing down, until I achieved something that was acceptable. It was then a question of super gluing the wings in the right place on the balsa fuselage, again with the aid of *DataFile Part 1* and the Mk XIVe. Once fitted, there were some pretty big gaps at the wing roots and I used some shaped plastic card to produce the distinctive curved fillets on the fuselage sides. But once filled and rubbed down, it all blended together. The model was now looking very much like one of the Spitfire family.

I next fitted the ICM tailplanes, before turning my thoughts to the rudder. This is quite a big beast on a Mk 17 and there was nothing in the spares box that would do, so it was scratch building time again. The size and shape, this time, came from the plans in DataFile Part 2, suitably scaled up from 1/72 to 1/48, and marked out on graph paper. The rudder was made from pieces of plastic card, sandwiched together, cut to shape and rubbed down. To create the effect of the horizontal ribbing I adapted a technique explained in an old edition of *SAMI* and stuck thin strips of Sellotape on to the rudder. I then painted on some undercoat, and, once it was dry, pulled off the Sellotape. This left slight variations in the surface, which, once the topcoat went on, would give the effect I was looking for. I used some off-cuts of plastic card and wire to make the stinger hook and its housing.

And then, it was just a question of adding the fiddly bits. Some work under the wings to make Airfix Mk V radiators sit flush on the wing raised them up enough to pass for the larger radiator and oil cooler of a Griffon-engined machine, and an old 1/76 tank track cut up provided a grill effect inside. I modified a Mk IX carburettor with plastic card and filler to represent the more open-mouthed version fitted to the Mk 17. Rear wheel and doors came from the spares box, as did the main gear, except I had to build the undercarriage legs from bits of plastic of suitable diameter, with thin strips of Tamiya tape for detail.

A few coats of Humbrol acrylic light grey as primer gave the various materials and colours a uniform appearance. It also made it look like a 'real' model, and more importantly to me, it actually did look like a Mk 17. I had decided, by this time, that I would produce the F Mk 17, not the FR Mk 17, to avoid having to make holes for the cameras of the latter version.

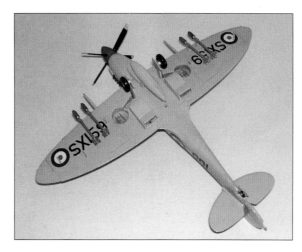

Centre-line fuel tank, rockets and aerials in place

Nose and Propeller

I toyed with creating the exhaust manifolds from scratch, but settled for fitting a spare set left over from a Monogram P-51D, on the basis that they were 6-stacks and would probably look fine on the completed model. The Griffon-engine's distinctive bulges over the cylinder heads on the cowling were the next challenge. I had nothing I could modify, so it really was a case of creating something from nothing.

For this I decided to try the crash moulding technique I'd read about in *SAMI* October 2007, using a bulldog clip, a wooden mitre block for support, a small candle and some plastic card. I used the parts from the Academy Mk XIVe, with a wooden handle held on by Blu-Tack, as the masters to push into the warmed plastic card. It worked, as I produced very passable copies. I didn't ruin the Academy parts - but only just, so I wouldn't recommend the direct moulding method again!

I had thought of using the same technique to create the spinner, by pushing in a Mk V version a bit more deeply, and then trimming to shape. This didn't work at all, as the plastic was too thin and brittle. The solution came from looking at the propeller unit as a whole. I had a spare Merlin 4-blade set from the Airfix Mk IX, but only Mk V 3-blade spinners. So, I twisted the blades around to face the other way (as Griffons rotate in the opposite direction from Merlins), and stuck them on their mounting to the Mk V back plate. I then put the Mk V spinner on top of the Mk IX blades, and glued where it touched. This left a gap between spinner and the back plate, into which I put some filler. Once dry and rubbed down, the result was a 4-blade propeller (admittedly with blades of the wrong profile) and the longer spinner of the Griffon.

Colour Scheme

While all of this was going on, I was pondering over the paint scheme and markings. I had been poring over quite a few photographs of Mk 17s, but none had the exact codes and serial numbers I could recreate from the decals in the spares box. Even if I had budgeted for some aftermarket decals, I couldn't actually find any suitable.

Although I wanted to recreate the high demarcation scheme, I was short of a pair of post-war roundels of a small enough size. For a camouflaged scheme, on the other hand, although I had plenty of wartime-style roundels, I had no white or yellow numbers of the right size and shape. The answer came with the lucky purchase of an Airfix Mk 46/47. When I opened up the box to see what treasures lay inside, I found that one of the Mk 47 schemes would not require its underwing roundels. So, I now had three pairs.

It was clear from looking at the photographic record that, even within the same squadron and ship, there seemed to be considerable variation in size, shape, style and location of markings used by the Fleet Air Arm on its Seafires. There was also variation in where the demarcation came between Sky and Extra Dark Sea Grey, at the wings, on the fuselage and on the tail. This was good for me, as it gave me the latitude to produce something representative.

So, the plan firmed up. I would model SX159, as if it had been on 1833 (RNVR) Naval Air Squadron's establishment in the mid-1950s. It would have the side number 166 and carry the BR tail codes of RNAS Bramcote. I had evidence for 1833 NAS aircraft in the high demarcation scheme with side numbers 157, 163 and 167, so it was reasonable to assume they had a 166 as well. My only real invention, therefore, would be the serial number. I could have researched further to find out exactly which aircraft had been on 1833 NAS's books, but that wasn't really the point of this project, and life's too short. I was,

after all, simply trying to make a representative aircraft from what I had available.

I decided that, in an attempt to distract the eye from any imperfections in the balsa fuselage, I would give it something else to look at. For this I used the centre-line drop tank provided in the Airfix Mk 46/47, which seemed to be fitted to a flight deck full of Seafire Mk 17s in a photograph I had seen. I also used the rockets from the same kit, as I had found a photograph of a 1833 NAS Mk 17, which showed the prominent carrying points for these weapons.

With the aid of photographs and *DataFile Part 2*, I marked and drilled the locating points for the rockets. I followed the guide in the Mk 46/47 instructions, and painted the heads red. I've read somewhere that this makes them concrete practice rounds, which sounds right for what 1833 NAS would have been doing. I first fitted all four rockets beneath each wing, as I reasoned that, if they could carry a 250lb bomb under each wing, then mathematically Mk 17s could carry four 60lb rockets. It looked fantastic! However, subsequent reading of the references has made me realise that Mk 17s only carried two on each wing, so I will have to snip off the lower set. But the model still bristles with underwing stores, and, with its pilot in the cockpit and the canopy slid back, looks ready to launch for an operational sortie.

Conclusion

And there we have it: a model from nothing, for (almost) nothing. It's not perfect, particularly around the nose and the tail, and its markings are an invention, but, to my mind, it does look like a Fleet Air Arm Seafire F Mk 17 from all angles, and it even has that distinctive hunched look around the cockpit, so my personal objective has been achieved. More importantly, the planning, problem-solving and completion of this project gave me an enormous amount of satisfaction, possibly more so than from putting together a plastic kit out of the box. For me, it sums up what modelling is all about : creation and enjoyment.

And the next project ? I'll probably take a rest from the multi-media world but I've got plenty of balsa left and, in the way that snooker players are always thinking a few shots ahead, I'm already working out what can I do with the spare wings from the Mk 46/47. They could come together with another balsa fuselage to stay as a Mk 46, to use the decals from the kit, or be cross-kitted with an Academy Mk XIVc for a Mk 45 or a Spitfire Mk 21. But that would leave me with a spare C wing… which could be matched with some ICM nose panels or a Merlin engine and balsa to make …

SUPERMARINE SEAFIRE F.XVII

Scale: 1/48

Kit No: 06102

Type: Injection Moulded Plastic

Manufacturer: Airfix

Seventeen Up

85

Airfix's New Tool Supermarine Seafire F.XVII
By David Francis

I have always like late mark Seafires, there is something about the post war classic Extra Dark Sea Grey over Sky that just looks classy. So, even though 1/48 is not my normal scale I was pleased to be given the opportunity to build the latest new-tool kit from Airfix.

On opening the box you will find it packed with light blue plastic just like the first Spitfire kit from the 1950s. What has changed is the level of detail in areas like the cockpit, which is almost equal to the best of Japanese kits. What has also changed are the panel lines, which used to be raised on older Airfix kits but are now engraved. These are probably the biggest weakness on the kit as though they are thin the engraving is very deep. Not a big problem, as it would be simple to fill them with Mr Surfacer, removing any excess with Mr Color thinner to produce a more realistic flush look to the model, but on this build what you see is what you get.

Two sets of wings are supplied, either ready for flight or folded, a nice feature that I wish all naval subjects could have, and whatever option you choose you also have separate control surfaces and dropped flaps. The instructions are typical Airfix with colour notes to the Humbrol colour range. OK in the UK but a real pain for anyone else. The markings are shown in colour profile with very clear placement guides and this brings me to one of the real strong points with this new kit - the decals. These have been a weak area on some recent Airfix kits but not this one, as they are beautifully printed by Cartograf and are the equal to any aftermarket product.

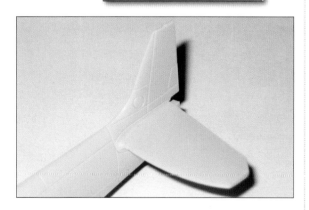

Can you spot the joint? A beautiful fit of parts is evident in many places on this kit

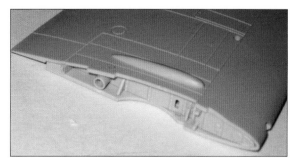

Wing fold detail out of the box is quite good

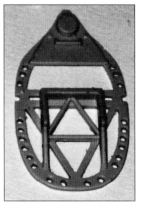

It does not take long to drill out the holes on the bulkhead frame, and is well worth the effort expended

I broke the top off the control column so replaced it with wire.

Two complete sets of wings are supplied – a real bonus, as 'optional' wingfolds rarely fit in the spread position

The Build

We start with the cockpit and this is made up from ten parts, including items like the throttle and height adjustment lever for the pilot's seat. The panel features some nice detail but I used Aeroscale's 1/48 UK instruments and universal placard decals to really jazz this area up. Another aftermarket addition was Eduard's Q-type belts (ED49007). This pre-painted set supplies four seat belts, and these are far better than anything I can paint.

One small modification I made was to drill out the recessed lightening holes on parts 90 and 33; this only takes a few minutes but really adds to the look of the cockpit.

At this point you can join the fuselage halves and the fit of parts is very good with only a small touch of filler needed on the spine to hide the join. Now is the time to decide on which wing configuration to use. I wanted to do the folded option so missed out opening any of the holes for the armament or fuel tanks. My reasoning was that the Seafire wings are folded manually so it is unlikely that these would be attached with the wings in the folded position. I assembled all the different sections, including the flaps, which I attached in the raised position as I found few photographs of these in the lowered position with the wings folded. I also chose not to fit the centre line fuel tanks so again did not drill out the mounting points but I did remember to fit the under fuselage ID lights before attaching the centre section to the fuselage. Again the fit was almost perfect with just a small amount of PVA needed to fill the seams, though I did need to do a little bit of sanding to make the rear joint perfect.

Once all the wing parts are assembled these were put aside for painting. The rest of the assembly proceeded rapidly as most parts just clipped into place, and the only area that needed any work was the two-part intake under the nose that required some Mr Surfacer to eradicate the seam. Parts are supplied to mount the undercarriage in either the raised or lowered position and you also have a choice of weighted or unweighted wheels, plus separate hubs, which makes painting easy. It was at this point I started the painting and the point at which I excelled by making two muck ups rather than my normal one.

Painting and Decals

Two main canopies are supplied, one to fit in the closed position and one with a different profile if you want to mount the canopy open. I temporarily attached the closed hood to the model with PVA to mask the cockpit and then made masks for the open canopy and windshield.

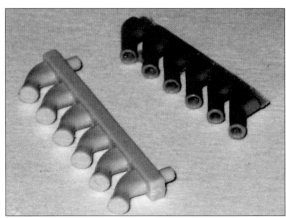

Kit exhaust stacks were replaced by hollow Quickboost items

Hard to believe this is not an aftermarket cockpit

Aeroscale's instrument decals really improve the kit's panel

Eduard seatbelts are better than anything I could paint, and are a welcome addition to any kit

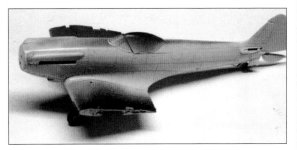
Painting under way. Pre-shading with black filled up the panel lines a little

For my mask I used Tamiya tape. Once applied to the clear parts the moulded detail shows through the tape if you hold it over a bright light. I then use a new number 11 blade to cut away the excess, making a perfect mask. It was at this point I had my first blunder as I knocked the main canopy onto the floor. No - it's not the parts-eating carpet but my size 9 foot that did the damage, as I then promptly trod on it with a resounding crack. Luckily a quick plea to the kind folk at Hornby, with an explanation, had a new canopy to me within 48 hours for which I am extremely grateful.

The kit supplies three markings options:

- 800 NAS, *HMS Triumph*, 1947. This option is shown in Sky and Extra Dark Sea Grey but many believe it should have a camouflaged finish with Slate Grey as the third colour
- 714 NAS, Air Warfare School. Sky with Extra Dark Sea Grey and Slate Grey, with large areas of yellow on the control surfaces and wing tips
- 1832 NAS, RNVR, Culham, 1950. My choice in the Extra Dark Sea Grey over Sky scheme

87

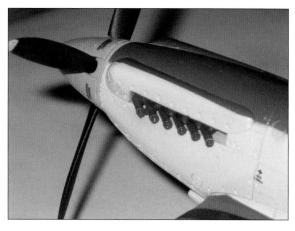

The slightly over-heavy engraving is the only downside, but does not detract from an attractive finished model

Muck-up number two. When painting the wings remember how they fold. I managed to paint the tips the wrong way round, with sky on top, and it was only when I was attaching them to the model that I realised. OOPS - a quick repaint and all was well. The spinner and blades were painted Humbrol 24 Trainer Yellow and once dry I masked the tips with Tamiya tape before painting the rest of the blades black.

Applying the markings was simple thanks to the clear instructions and high quality decals, but if you have chosen the folded wing option you may have to do some strategic cutting.

Final Bits

The folded wings were now attached to the model, and the use of the supplied locking brace makes gluing at the correct angle simple though I did need to remove a small amount of plastic from the wing tip's mounting lug to get a positive fit. The pitot tube and underwing aerials were now added, though I replaced the latter with thin metal rod from Albion alloys both for strength and scale appearance as the plastic parts are quite thick.

The arrestor hook can be mounted either raised, with the hook retracted, or lowered with the hook extended. I decided the extended version added some interest so went with that, though to date I have broken the hook off at least four times. The exhaust stacks have solid ends and I started to drill them out, but on number five I went a bit off course and spoilt the part, so on my model the kit parts have been replaced with Quickboost exhausts intended for a Hasegawa Mk IX (QB48138), which are a simple way to add detail for those like me with shaky hands.

To finish the cockpit, canopies were added to the model using PVA, and the only thing to remember here is to fix the inner internal armoured glass (C5) before you attach the windshield and remember to use the correct canopy for the open or closed position.

Conclusion

I am no Seafire expert and though the panel lines are a bit overdone for my tastes the model appears to match the photographs of the type very well. This kit has provided one of the most enjoyable modelling

experiences that I have ever had from an Airfix kit and I highly recommend this kit to all levels of modelling experience, and as a testament I have opened my wallet and laid down another example, plus the recent Freightdog Seafire sheet so I can build one with spread wings and a full weapons fit. I know I swore this New Year that there would be no more 1/48 kits but this one was just so much fun that I simply couldn't resist.

Chapter X

H.P. 42 "HERACLES"
Scale: 1/144
Kit No: 03172
Type: *Injection Moulded Plastic*
Manufacturer: *Airfix*

Airfix Kit 03172

Steady as the Rock of Gibraltar

Airfix's 1/144 veteran Handley Page HP 42

'Steady as the Rock of Gibraltar...and almost as fast'

By Neil Pinchbeck

I don't know who coined this witticism about Frederick Handley Page's famous 1930s four-engined biplane airliner, but it does capture the range of opinion about the aircraft. Some writers wax lyrical about the HP 42 as an innovative and groundbreaking piece of aeronautical history. Others regard it as a dinosaur, serving only the limited needs of Imperial Airways.

With its biplane format and a tail empennage little changed from

This kit was the 1994 'Classic Airliners' reissue which thankfully retained Roy Cross's wonderful artwork, albeit in reduced form

its WW1 forebears, the HP 42 was hardly innovative in the purely aerodynamic sense. It was groundbreaking though, in that it was designed, in great detail, to transport passengers in safety and comfort, not to say luxury. As such, and with its fabled reliability, it was to popularise air travel in the public mind and so pave the way for the future (*Heracles* was the first airliner to clock up one million miles flown, and in 1935 was airborne on 361 of the 365 days of the year).

Personally, I like to think of it as a dinosaur. It has that same massive presence and stately grace. And, of course, dinosaurs were immensely successful in their day.

The Kit

I believe that Airfix first released their 1/144 HP 42 in the early 1960s, and I expect that boxing is fetching collectors' prices by now. A misleading feature of both boxes is that the title could lead you to believe that *Heracles* was the aircraft's type name. In fact it was simply Handley Page HP 42. Eight were built, all for Imperial Airways, and all with individual names from history and mythology beginning with 'H' (see below). *Heracles* (G-AAXC) and *Helena* (G-AAXF) have always

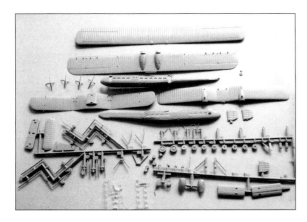

Despite the small scale the impression is of plenty of plastic for your money and good crisp detail

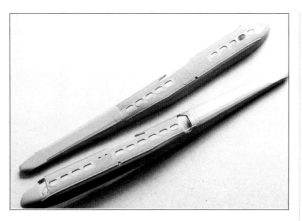

The corrugated ribs of the Duralumin fuselage skin look right

The injected wiindow panels are thick and do not bode well

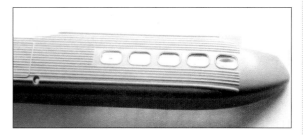

Sink marks further sistort the thick plastic

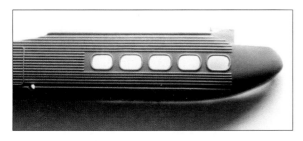

Wiindows were eventually replaces with acetate strip

Interior detail began with a fuselage floor

91

been the two alternatives offered on the Airfix decal sheet.

What constitutes good detail at this scale is an interesting point. The corrugated ribs of the Duralumin fuselage skin are not numerically accurate, but I think they look right and Airfix made the right decision. The fabric-covered areas at the rear of the fuselage are also very nicely done.

See-through Decision

I haven't made an airliner for quite a while, but I remember one of the first things to decide is how much interior detail to include. To a large extent this is governed by how much will be visible. Thick, injection-moulded window panels do not bode well. Worse still, when they are inserted sink marks give a distorted lens effect which will destroy any real visibility. I tried replacing these with a simple strip of thin clear PVC sheet. Ah, much better!

Insider Dealing

Having made sure that there was a reasonable chance of some things being visible, it was now time to indulge in one of the most enjoyable bits of our hobby — getting completely carried away!

Things began with a fuselage floor and the interesting cranked bulkhead dividing crew and passenger compartments. I painted curtains on the inside of my PVC window strip. Seats were made from 'L' section plastistrut; tables from 'T' section. Cabin interiors were mahogany panelled, embellished with gold decoration. On the original aircraft flowered chintz covered the well-upholstered seats and there was deep pile carpet underfoot.

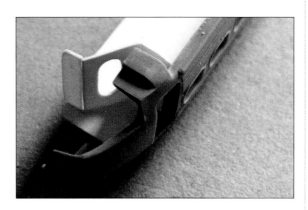

The interesting cranked bulkhead dividing crew and passenger compartments

The cockpit was also furnished with seats, again made from 'L' section. I also made control panels and wheel-type control. All of this then began to creep backwards!

The midships section was taken up with a luggage and cargo bay on the starboard side. To port were two toilets, and a steward's pantry, which opened onto a bar area. Between these, a corridor linked the two saloons. This layout was to keep the passenger seating as far away from engine noise as possible. Of the eight HP 42s built, four — *Heracles, Horatius, Hengist* and *Helena* —were finished thus, as Croydon-based HP 42Ws, in what was known as the 'Western' layout for European services. (The names *Hecate* and *Hesperides* had originally been chosen, but were rejected because of the hellfire

Painted curtains on the inside of the PVC window strip. Seats were made from 'L' section plastistrut; tables from 'T' section

Control panels and wheel-type control columns were scratchbuilt

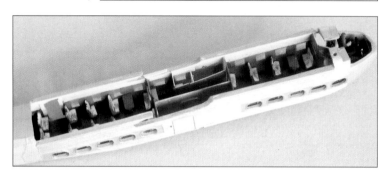

The passenger accommodation was divided into two saloons or cars (the HP 42 was seen as a direct rival to Pullman train services)

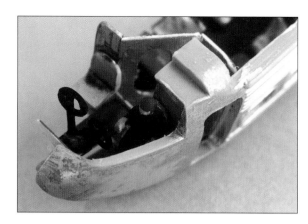

The cockpit was also furnished with seats, again made from 'L' section.

The figures are 1/150 (what's 1/3,600th between friends?) architectural accessories by Graham Avis Details and I got them from 4D Models of Leman Street, London — you can find them on the Internet

Some of you may have your suspicions about the identity of the gentleman with the large moustaches in the rear saloon, but more of him later. Note the bloodstain…

implications of the former and the prospect of Imperial's staff having repeatedly to spell-out the latter on documents. *Hannibal*, *Horsa*, *Hanno* and *Hadrian* were HP 42E 'Eastern' variants, based at Cairo for Empire routes to India and Africa, and featured an enlarged midships cargo bay and much reduced seating.

Figuratively Speaking

You may have noticed that, as part of getting carried away, the model is beginning to be peopled by small figures. These are 1/150 scale (what's 1/3,600th between friends?) architectural accessories by Graham Avis Details and I got them from 4D Models of Leman Street, London — you can find them on the Internet.

Some of you may have your suspicions about the identity of the gentleman with the large moustaches in the rear saloon, but more of him later.

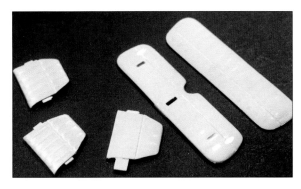

Preparing the tail components and filling ejector pin marksT

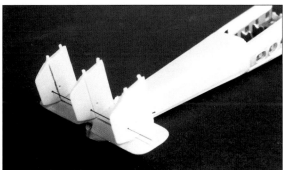
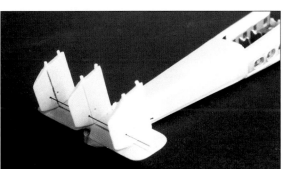

The three vertical fins and rudders were set in place

The Tail

Whilst preparing the tail components and filling ejector pin marks, I realised that the whole biplane tail empennage was very complicated and would take some sorting out. Since there are no HP 42s to go and look at, the next best thing was a visit to the Science Museum, South Kensington, and a look at their large-scale HP 42 model, which was a great help.

I started by fixing the lower horizontal plane to the fuselage. The three vertical fins and rudders were then set in place. The rudders were pre-drilled to receive the link bar, which was made from a brush bristle.

At the Science Museum, I noticed that that the upper horizontal plane does not actually touch the fins. I used small bits of rod stock as spacers at the fin fronts and rudder-post positions. Next, the outer rudder balances went on and cross bracing, with brush bristles, began. With the bracing complete, the upper plane was set in place. I finished by adding the elevator control horns and wires.

Bumps, Ridges and Wings

A common problem with vintage biplane kits is the portrayal of the ribbed structure of flying surfaces in general and rib tapes in particular. These are usually exaggerated, often to the point where they spoil the whole model.

Although I have seen worse, this kit does share this problem. It is

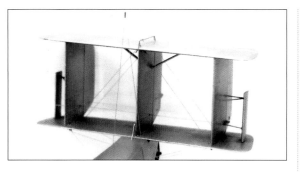

he Science Museum's large-scale HP 42 model was a great help

The outer rudder balances went on and cross bracing, with brush bristles, began

Adding the elevator control horns and wires

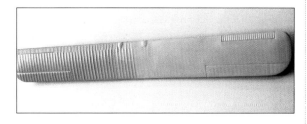

Heavy ribbing is evident on this kit (left). The best solution here was simply to sand off the ridges (right)

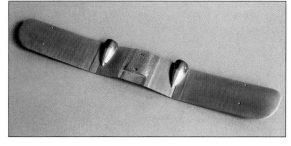

The final coat of aluminium was very lightly rubbed down with 1500 grit wet 'n' dry before sealing with a coat of Klear

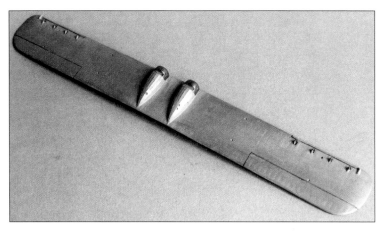

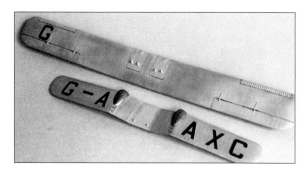

The wings were decalled at this point

The forward part of each engine nacelle was painted with MetalCote steel (27003)

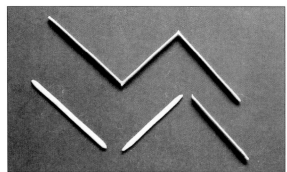

The kit struts were seperated for a better scale appearance

The next job was cleaning up the engine parts

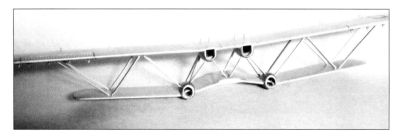

The resulting gain in accuracy of appearance was worth the effort

Engines were painted various shades of MetalCote and assembled

made worse here since contemporary photographs show that the HP 42 had particularly smooth flying surfaces, with the structure only just visible, especially from any distance. I decided the best solution here was simply to sand off the ridges until the undulations were only just visible. The exception was the leading-edge slats, which seem to have been metal and quite ridged, so I left these.

This done, the wings were painted with two coats of Humbrol MetalCote polished aluminium (27002). You can't over-paint MetalCote, so a coat of Johnson's Klear went between the paint coats. The final coat of aluminium was very lightly rubbed down with 1500 grit wet 'n' dry before sealing with a coat of Klear. The forward part of each engine nacelle was painted with MetalCote steel (27003).

I decided to decal the wings at this point since they wouldn't be very accessible later on. You will also see that I added fuel tank vent pipes and aileron control horns and wires to the upper surface of the upper wing.

'Flying Forth Bridge'

The wings of the HP 42 had Warren girder bracing, that is to say that the interplane struts sloped or angled in such a way as to bear all the flight stresses, making bracing wires unnecessary and leading to the nickname 'Flying Forth Bridge'. In the kit this is portrayed by continuous interplane struts. On the real aircraft these struts passed through the wing surface, to meet structural elements inside the wing. This meant that there was actually a gap of several inches between the bases of the struts, at the wing surface. For this reason I decided to separate the struts. Thus all the struts had to be set in place individually, which was rather fiddly, but I think the resulting gain in accuracy of appearance was worth the effort.

Engines and Props

The next job was cleaning up the engine parts. This done, they were painted various shades of MetalCote and assembled. It is difficult to tell from black-and-white photographs what the finish was for the propellers. Once again, I took my cue from the Science Museum model and painted them aluminium doped. The engines were then set in place on the wing unit. The last job of wing construction was adding the only two bracing wires between the outer pair of interplane struts.

Undercarriage

The large circle of plastic through which the axle passes is a work of fiction, which is best minimised by shaping. Otherwise, the undercarriage parts aren't bad for basic accuracy. Before the fixed

The engines were set in place on the wing unit

The last job of wing construction was adding the only two bracing wires between the outer pair of interplane struts

Once again, a cue was taken from The Science Museum's model

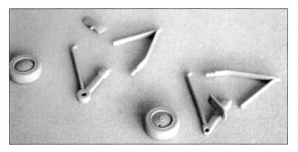

The large circle of plastic through which the axle passes is best minimised by shaping

A little packing was necessary on the port side, to get everything square

undercarriage legs can go on, the wing unit had to be fixed in place. A little packing was necessary on the port side, to get everything square. HP 42 tyres seem to have been quite low pressure, so I gave mine quite a flat surface to sit on before painting and the adding of bracing wires to legs and mudguards.

Finishing Off

HP 42s sported quite an array of small external features. Researched from photographs, mine were scratchbuilt and include radio mast, wind generator and pitot head. My co-pilot salutes the ensign from his hatch.* The ensign is painted on aluminium kitchen foil and fixed to the mast with fine copper wire. I made the stairways from plastistrut.

A Tale of Two Mysteries

It seems ironical that such a stolid character as the HP 42 should be associated with two famous mysteries. Many will have guessed that my character in the rear saloon is none other than Hercule Poirot. In her 1935 masterpiece *Death in the Clouds*, Agatha Christie avoids referring to the HP 42 by name (probably for legal reasons), but the descriptions and seating diagram leave no room for doubt. I couldn't resist a large bloodstain to mark the seat of Madam Giselle. If you don't know how this came about, I will leave you with a good read. The Belgian detective's 'little grey cells' will reveal all!

From fiction to fact. The second mystery concerns the disappearance of Hannibal (G-AAGX) in March 1940. On the return trip from Karachi to Alexandria, while routing Jask-Sharjah, the aircraft simply vanished over the Gulf of Oman. No satisfactory cause or explanation has ever emerged for the disappearance of the aircraft and its eight passengers and crew — the only losses in more than 100,000 flying hours and 10 million air miles jointly flown by the HP 42 fleet.

95

HP 42 tyres seem to have been quite low pressure

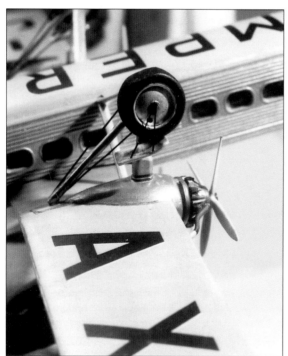

Radio mast, wind generator and pitot head were scratchbuilt

Extinction of the Dinosaurs

By early 1941, all eight HP 42s had been destroyed. With the exception of *Hannibal*, all were accounted for by ground fires, gales or other adverse weather conditions. The last survivor was *Helena*, whose fuselage served as an office at RNAS Donibristle. So it was that the dinosaurs became extinct. It seems fitting to me that they should have succumbed to such elemental forces.

* *Apocryphal story has it that one redoubtable Imperial Airways captain, a former Royal Naval Air Service pilot, on several times repeating the order "Haul down the ensign" to his First Officer to no avail, was heard throughout the forward cabin to bellow, 'Mister, get that bloody rag in!'*

Passengers boarding an H.P.42W at Croydon, bound for Paris-Le Bourget. Note the covered walkway, a forerunner of modern boarding 'gates'. The H.P.42's banana-shaped fuselage sat low enough for steps not to be needed

Speed Without Hurry

By Mike Jerram
All photographs: Mike Jerram Collection

Passengers called them 'flying bananas'. Pilot from rival airlines, feeling smug in their sleek new Douglases and Lockheeds, made unkind remarks about aeroplanes with built-in headwinds. Yet, for all the ribaldry, Imperial Airways' slow and stately 'aerial galleons', their Handley Page HP 42 biplanes, won envied reputations for safety, dependability, passenger comfort and service.

The HP 42 was spawned in the spring of 1928 when Imperial, then Britain's 'flag carrier' airline, invited aircraft manufacturers to tender for the supply of a fleet of new aeroplanes for the Empire air mail route to India, stipulating that the aircraft should offer 'the greatest safety, highest possible payload capacity and lowest costs of operation' and have a stalling speed not above 52 mph. Beyond that, tendering companies were allowed 'the greatest possible freedom of expression for their own ideas'.

Handley Page Ltd's tenders for four Eastern route and four Western route (services within Europe) aircraft were accepted, and in July 1929 a fully furnished wooden fuselage mock-up of the aircraft was displayed at the Aero exhibition at Olympia, London, where its Pullman-style interior, complete with cocktail bar, drew much approving comment.

The prototype HP 42 made its first flight from the Handley Page factory airfield at Radlett, Hertfordshire on 14 November 1930. Three days later it was demonstrated to the press, getting off the ground after

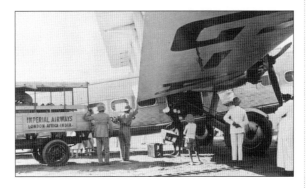

(above and opposite top) Passengers disembarking and freight going aboard an H.P.42E at Khartoum during a stopover en route to South Africa

The captain of H.P.42W G-AAXC Heracles transmitting on the Marconi radio equipment installed in Imperial's H.P.42s. Note the ship-sized control wheel

97

H.P.42W G-AAXF Helena is one of the options offered on the Airfix kit's decal sheet

G-AAGX Hannibal was an H.P.42E, used on Imperial Airways' Empire route to India and Africa

a take-off run of just 60 yards and giving an impressive demonstration with three of its four Bristol Jupiter radial engines throttled back.

Despite its apparent outdatedness, with heavy Warren girder strut bracing and triple-finned biplane tail unit, the HP 42 made up for its lack of external beauty with elegant comforts within. The slight 'kink' in its fuselage profile (hence the 'flying banana' nickname) brought the passenger door close to the ground, so that steps were not needed, and once passengers entered its cabin they found inlaid wood panelling, comfortable armchairs, long picture windows, two lavatories, duplicate instruments on which they could follow the flight's progress, and individual heating and ventilation controls for each seat. The galley, lavatories and baggage compartment were sited between the two passenger saloons in an area adjacent to the four engines, thus further reducing noise levels in the soundproofed cabins, while thoughtful use of anhedralled centre-sections to the lower wings enabled the wing/fuselage junctions to be placed above the passenger saloon's ceiling so that travellers might enjoy an unimpaired view of the passing landscape.

HP 42E 'Eastern' variants for service on the India and South Africa Empire routes were powered by 550 hp Bristol Jupiter XI.F engines, while HP 42W 'Western' aircraft for the London-Paris cross-channel shuttle and other continental services had Jupiter X.FBMs. The 'Es' carried twelve passengers in each forward and aft saloon, while the 'Ws', which had reduced baggage space for short-haul operations, carried twenty and eighteen passengers respectively in fore and aft cabins. The operational crew comprised a captain, first officer, radio officer and one or two stewards.

On 11 June 1931 it fell to one of the Eastern aircraft, *Hannibal*, to inaugurate the London-Paris 'Silver Wing' service from Croydon to Le Bourget, before journeying to its permanent base at Cairo in the following August. By early 1932 all eight HP 42s were in service with Imperial Airways, and the Western aircraft were a familiar sight at Croydon, where their short take-off and landing characteristics enabled them to operate in moderate winds directly from the Customs apron

rather than the grass airfield proper. While the 600-foot take-off run and 65 mph landing speed of the HP 42 could be an asset, its slow-speed performance was also its Achilles' heel when facing a brisk headwind, which would eat into its leisurely 95 mph cruising speed. One former Imperial Airways captain recalled taking more than an hour to traverse the narrowest stretch of the English Channel while en route to Paris on a particularly breezy day.

Nonetheless, for a fare of £6 15s 0d (£6.75) the HP 42s proved immensely popular with businessmen and well-heeled travellers. Passengers departed from the Airways Terminus at London's Victoria Station at 8.15 am or 11.45 am and arrived at the Hotel Boby-Lafayette on rue Lafayette in the heart of the French capital three hours and forty five minutes later. En route they were served breakfast or lunch, the latter accompanied by fresh vegetables and fine wines. Speed without Hurry was Imperial's motto. Their boast that 'a complete service of meals — breakfast, lunch and tea — is served on the flight between London and Paris' was unfortunately worded, however, and drew from C G Grey, waspish Editor of *The Aeroplane* magazine, the wry comment that he 'had no idea that the distance was so great, or alternatively that Imperial Airways' big four-engined airliners took so long to get there'. Whilst there was food and drink aplenty, smoking on board was strictly forbidden, as one passenger found to his cost when he was fined £10 by Croydon magistrates after lighting up an after-lunch cigar aboard *Heracles*. Smoking apart, Imperial's passengers were always right. A senior HP 42 captain was summarily dismissed for being (probably justifiably) rude to an especially tiresome and demanding passenger.

In Europe HP 42s eventually ranged beyond Paris to Brussels, Basle, Cologne and Zurich, and were in great demand at home for day trips to events such as the Grand National horse race and for joyriding, including 'tea flights' over central London. The Eastern HP 42s flew out of Cairo to Karachi and Delhi en route to South Africa. The journey from England to India took six-and-a-half days with night stops en route. On these long-hauls a close rapport grew between passengers and crew. It was not unusual for an HP 42 captain to dine with his charges, nor was he above asking them to help refuel the aeroplane on those occasions when it became necessary to make a stop at one of Imperial's unattended desert fuel stores.

Utilisation was high. *Heracles* flew more than 1.3 million miles (at 95 mph remember!) and carried 160,000 passengers in eight years' service, at a time when air travel was largely restricted to the middle and upper classes.

Ironically, despite five- or six-fold increases in airliner cruise speeds since the HP 42s made their stately way across the English Channel, more than seventy years later, thanks to security measures, airways routings and surface transport delays you'd now be very hard-pressed to match Imperial's total journey time between central London and the grands boulevards of Paris.

Contemporary Imperial Airways advertisements for the London-Paris Silver Wing service and the Empire route